HEBREW
VOCABULARY

FOR ENGLISH SPEAKERS

ENGLISH-HEBREW

The most useful words
To expand your lexicon and sharpen
your language skills

5000 words

Hebrew vocabulary for English speakers - 5000 words
By Andrey Taranov

T&P Books vocabularies are intended for helping you learn, memorize and review foreign words. The dictionary is divided into themes, covering all major spheres of everyday activities, business, science, culture, etc.

The process of learning words using T&P Books' theme-based dictionaries gives you the following advantages:

- Correctly grouped source information predetermines success at subsequent stages of word memorization
- Availability of words derived from the same root allowing memorization of word units (rather than separate words)
- Small units of words facilitate the process of establishing associative links needed for consolidation of vocabulary
- Level of language knowledge can be estimated by the number of learned words

Copyright © 2016 T&P Books Publishing

All rights reserved. No part of this book may be reproduced or utilized in any form or by any means, electronic or mechanical, including photocopying, recording or by information storage and retrieval system, without permission in writing from the publishers.

T&P Books Publishing
www.tpbooks.com

ISBN: 978-1-78716-412-3

This book is also available in E-book formats.
Please visit www.tpbooks.com or the major online bookstores.

HEBREW VOCABULARY
for English speakers

T&P Books vocabularies are intended to help you learn, memorize, and review foreign words. The vocabulary contains over 5000 commonly used words arranged thematically.

- Vocabulary contains the most commonly used words
- Recommended as an addition to any language course
- Meets the needs of beginners and advanced learners of foreign languages
- Convenient for daily use, revision sessions, and self-testing activities
- Allows you to assess your vocabulary

Special features of the vocabulary

- Words are organized according to their meaning, not alphabetically
- Words are presented in three columns to facilitate the reviewing and self-testing processes
- Words in groups are divided into small blocks to facilitate the learning process
- The vocabulary offers a convenient and simple transcription of each foreign word

The vocabulary has 155 topics including:

Basic Concepts, Numbers, Colors, Months, Seasons, Units of Measurement, Clothing & Accessories, Food & Nutrition, Restaurant, Family Members, Relatives, Character, Feelings, Emotions, Diseases, City, Town, Sightseeing, Shopping, Money, House, Home, Office, Working in the Office, Import & Export, Marketing, Job Search, Sports, Education, Computer, Internet, Tools, Nature, Countries, Nationalities and more ...

T&P BOOKS' THEME-BASED DICTIONARIES

The Correct System for Memorizing Foreign Words

Acquiring vocabulary is one of the most important elements of learning a foreign language, because words allow us to express our thoughts, ask questions, and provide answers. An inadequate vocabulary can impede communication with a foreigner and make it difficult to understand a book or movie well.

The pace of activity in all spheres of modern life, including the learning of modern languages, has increased. Today, we need to memorize large amounts of information (grammar rules, foreign words, etc.) within a short period. However, this does not need to be difficult. All you need to do is to choose the right training materials, learn a few special techniques, and develop your individual training system.

Having a system is critical to the process of language learning. Many people fail to succeed in this regard; they cannot master a foreign language because they fail to follow a system comprised of selecting materials, organizing lessons, arranging new words to be learned, and so on. The lack of a system causes confusion and eventually, lowers self-confidence.

T&P Books' theme-based dictionaries can be included in the list of elements needed for creating an effective system for learning foreign words. These dictionaries were specially developed for learning purposes and are meant to help students effectively memorize words and expand their vocabulary.

Generally speaking, the process of learning words consists of three main elements:

- Reception (creation or acquisition) of a training material, such as a word list
- Work aimed at memorizing new words
- Work aimed at reviewing the learned words, such as self-testing

All three elements are equally important since they determine the quality of work and the final result. All three processes require certain skills and a well-thought-out approach.

New words are often encountered quite randomly when learning a foreign language and it may be difficult to include them all in a unified list. As a result, these words remain written on scraps of paper, in book margins, textbooks, and so on. In order to systematize such words, we have to create and continually update a "book of new words." A paper notebook, a netbook, or a tablet PC can be used for these purposes.

This "book of new words" will be your personal, unique list of words. However, it will only contain the words that you came across during the learning process. For example, you might have written down the words "Sunday," "Tuesday," and "Friday." However, there are additional words for days of the week, for example, "Saturday," that are missing, and your list of words would be incomplete. Using a theme dictionary, in addition to the "book of new words," is a reasonable solution to this problem.

The theme-based dictionary may serve as the basis for expanding your vocabulary.

It will be your big "book of new words" containing the most frequently used words of a foreign language already included. There are quite a few theme-based dictionaries available, and you should ensure that you make the right choice in order to get the maximum benefit from your purchase.

Therefore, we suggest using theme-based dictionaries from T&P Books Publishing as an aid to learning foreign words. Our books are specially developed for effective use in the sphere of vocabulary systematization, expansion and review.

Theme-based dictionaries are not a magical solution to learning new words. However, they can serve as your main database to aid foreign-language acquisition. Apart from theme dictionaries, you can have copybooks for writing down new words, flash cards, glossaries for various texts, as well as other resources; however, a good theme dictionary will always remain your primary collection of words.

T&P Books' theme-based dictionaries are specialty books that contain the most frequently used words in a language.

The main characteristic of such dictionaries is the division of words into themes. For example, the *City* theme contains the words "street," "crossroads," "square," "fountain," and so on. The *Talking* theme might contain words like "to talk," "to ask," "question," and "answer".

All the words in a theme are divided into smaller units, each comprising 3–5 words. Such an arrangement improves the perception of words and makes the learning process less tiresome. Each unit contains a selection of words with similar meanings or identical roots. This allows you to learn words in small groups and establish other associative links that have a positive effect on memorization.

The words on each page are placed in three columns: a word in your native language, its translation, and its transcription. Such positioning allows for the use of techniques for effective memorization. After closing the translation column, you can flip through and review foreign words, and vice versa. "This is an easy and convenient method of review – one that we recommend you do often."

Our theme-based dictionaries contain transcriptions for all the foreign words. Unfortunately, none of the existing transcriptions are able to convey the exact nuances of foreign pronunciation. That is why we recommend using the transcriptions only as a supplementary learning aid. Correct pronunciation can only be acquired with the help of sound. Therefore our collection includes audio theme-based dictionaries.

The process of learning words using T&P Books' theme-based dictionaries gives you the following advantages:

- You have correctly grouped source information, which predetermines your success at subsequent stages of word memorization
- Availability of words derived from the same root (lazy, lazily, lazybones), allowing you to memorize word units instead of separate words
- Small units of words facilitate the process of establishing associative links needed for consolidation of vocabulary
- You can estimate the number of learned words and hence your level of language knowledge
- The dictionary allows for the creation of an effective and high-quality revision process
- You can revise certain themes several times, modifying the revision methods and techniques
- Audio versions of the dictionaries help you to work out the pronunciation of words and develop your skills of auditory word perception

The T&P Books' theme-based dictionaries are offered in several variants differing in the number of words: 1.500, 3.000, 5.000, 7.000, and 9.000 words. There are also dictionaries containing 15,000 words for some language combinations. Your choice of dictionary will depend on your knowledge level and goals.

We sincerely believe that our dictionaries will become your trusty assistant in learning foreign languages and will allow you to easily acquire the necessary vocabulary.

TABLE OF CONTENTS

T&P Books' Theme-Based Dictionaries	4
Pronunciation guide	13
Abbreviations	14
BASIC CONCEPTS	15
Basic concepts. Part 1	15
1. Pronouns	15
2. Greetings. Salutations. Farewells	15
3. How to address	16
4. Cardinal numbers. Part 1	16
5. Cardinal numbers. Part 2	18
6. Ordinal numbers	18
7. Numbers. Fractions	18
8. Numbers. Basic operations	19
9. Numbers. Miscellaneous	19
10. The most important verbs. Part 1	20
11. The most important verbs. Part 2	20
12. The most important verbs. Part 3	21
13. The most important verbs. Part 4	22
14. Colors	23
15. Questions	24
16. Prepositions	25
17. Function words. Adverbs. Part 1	25
18. Function words. Adverbs. Part 2	27
Basic concepts. Part 2	29
19. Weekdays	29
20. Hours. Day and night	29
21. Months. Seasons	30
22. Units of measurement	32
23. Containers	33
HUMAN BEING	35
Human being. The body	35
24. Head	35
25. Human body	36

Clothing & Accessories 38

26. Outerwear. Coats 38
27. Men's & women's clothing 38
28. Clothing. Underwear 39
29. Headwear 39
30. Footwear 39
31. Personal accessories 40
32. Clothing. Miscellaneous 41
33. Personal care. Cosmetics 41
34. Watches. Clocks 42

Food. Nutricion 44

35. Food 44
36. Drinks 46
37. Vegetables 47
38. Fruits. Nuts 47
39. Bread. Candy 48
40. Cooked dishes 49
41. Spices 50
42. Meals 50
43. Table setting 51
44. Restaurant 51

Family, relatives and friends 53

45. Personal information. Forms 53
46. Family members. Relatives 53

Medicine 55

47. Diseases 55
48. Symptoms. Treatments. Part 1 56
49. Symptoms. Treatments. Part 2 57
50. Symptoms. Treatments. Part 3 58
51. Doctors 59
52. Medicine. Drugs. Accessories 59

HUMAN HABITAT 61
City 61

53. City. Life in the city 61
54. Urban institutions 62
55. Signs 64
56. Urban transportation 65

57.	Sightseeing	66
58.	Shopping	66
59.	Money	67
60.	Post. Postal service	68

Dwelling. House. Home — 70

61.	House. Electricity	70
62.	Villa. Mansion	70
63.	Apartment	71
64.	Furniture. Interior	71
65.	Bedding	72
66.	Kitchen	72
67.	Bathroom	73
68.	Household appliances	74

HUMAN ACTIVITIES — 76
Job. Business. Part 1 — 76

69.	Office. Working in the office	76
70.	Business processes. Part 1	77
71.	Business processes. Part 2	78
72.	Production. Works	79
73.	Contract. Agreement	81
74.	Import & Export	81
75.	Finances	82
76.	Marketing	83
77.	Advertising	83
78.	Banking	84
79.	Telephone. Phone conversation	85
80.	Cell phone	85
81.	Stationery	86
82.	Kinds of business	86

Job. Business. Part 2 — 89

83.	Show. Exhibition	89
84.	Science. Research. Scientists	90

Professions and occupations — 92

85.	Job search. Dismissal	92
86.	Business people	92
87.	Service professions	94
88.	Military professions and ranks	94
89.	Officials. Priests	95

90.	Agricultural professions	96
91.	Art professions	96
92.	Various professions	97
93.	Occupations. Social status	98

Education 100

94.	School	100
95.	College. University	101
96.	Sciences. Disciplines	102
97.	Writing system. Orthography	102
98.	Foreign languages	104

Rest. Entertainment. Travel 106

99.	Trip. Travel	106
100.	Hotel	107

TECHNICAL EQUIPMENT. TRANSPORTATION 108
Technical equipment 108

101.	Computer	108
102.	Internet. E-mail	109
103.	Electricity	110
104.	Tools	111

Transportation 114

105.	Airplane	114
106.	Train	115
107.	Ship	116
108.	Airport	118

Life events 119

109.	Holidays. Event	119
110.	Funerals. Burial	120
111.	War. Soldiers	121
112.	War. Military actions. Part 1	122
113.	War. Military actions. Part 2	123
114.	Weapons	125
115.	Ancient people	126
116.	Middle Ages	127
117.	Leader. Chief. Authorities	129
118.	Breaking the law. Criminals. Part 1	129
119.	Breaking the law. Criminals. Part 2	131

120.	Police. Law. Part 1	132
121.	Police. Law. Part 2	133

NATURE
The Earth. Part 1

122.	Outer space	135
123.	The Earth	136
124.	Cardinal directions	137
125.	Sea. Ocean	137
126.	Seas' and Oceans' names	138
127.	Mountains	139
128.	Mountains names	140
129.	Rivers	140
130.	Rivers' names	141
131.	Forest	142
132.	Natural resources	143

The Earth. Part 2

133.	Weather	145
134.	Severe weather. Natural disasters	146

Fauna

135.	Mammals. Predators	147
136.	Wild animals	147
137.	Domestic animals	149
138.	Birds	150
139.	Fish. Marine animals	151
140.	Amphibians. Reptiles	152
141.	Insects	152

Flora

142.	Trees	154
143.	Shrubs	155
144.	Fruits. Berries	155
145.	Flowers. Plants	156
146.	Cereals, grains	157

COUNTRIES. NATIONALITIES

147.	Western Europe	158
148.	Central and Eastern Europe	158
149.	Former USSR countries	159

150. Asia	159
151. North America	160
152. Central and South America	160
153. Africa	161
154. Australia. Oceania	161
155. Cities	161

PRONUNCIATION GUIDE

Letter's name	Letter	Hebrew example	T&P phonetic alphabet	English example
Alef	א	אריה	[ɑ], [ɑː]	bath, to pass
	א	אחד	[ɛ], [ɛː]	habit, bad
	א	מָאָה	[ʔ]	glottal stop
Bet	ב	בית	[b]	baby, book
Gimel	ג	גמל	[g]	game, gold
Gimel+geresh	ג׳	ג׳ונגל	[dʒ]	joke, general
Dalet	ד	דג	[d]	day, doctor
Hei	ה	הר	[h]	home, have
Vav	ו	וסת	[v]	very, river
Zayin	ז	זאב	[z]	zebra, please
Zayin+geresh	ז׳	ז׳ורנל	[ʒ]	forge, pleasure
Chet	ח	חוט	[x]	as in Scots 'loch'
Tet	ט	טוב	[t]	tourist, trip
Yud	י	יום	[j]	yes, New York
Kaph	ך כ	בריש	[k]	clock, kiss
Lamed	ל	לחם	[l]	lace, people
Mem	ם מ	מלך	[m]	magic, milk
Nun	ן נ	נר	[n]	name, normal
Samech	ס	סוס	[s]	city, boss
Ayin	ע	עין	[ɑ], [ɑː]	bath, to pass
	ע	תִשְעִים	[ʔ]	voiced pharyngeal fricative
Pei	ף פ	פיל	[p]	pencil, private
Tsadi	ץ צ	צעצוע	[ts]	cats, tsetse fly
Tsadi+geresh	ץ׳ צ׳	צ׳ק	[tʃ]	church, French
Qoph	ק	קוף	[k]	clock, kiss
Resh	ר	רכבת	[r]	French (guttural) R
Shin	ש	שלחן, עָשְׂרִים	[s], [ʃ]	city, machine
Tav	ת	תפוז	[t]	tourist, trip

ABBREVIATIONS
used in the vocabulary

English abbreviations

ab.	-	about
adj	-	adjective
adv	-	adverb
anim.	-	animate
as adj	-	attributive noun used as adjective
e.g.	-	for example
etc.	-	et cetera
fam.	-	familiar
fem.	-	feminine
form.	-	formal
inanim.	-	inanimate
masc.	-	masculine
math	-	mathematics
mil.	-	military
n	-	noun
pl	-	plural
pron.	-	pronoun
sb	-	somebody
sing.	-	singular
sth	-	something
v aux	-	auxiliary verb
vi	-	intransitive verb
vi, vt	-	intransitive, transitive verb
vt	-	transitive verb

Hebrew abbreviations

ז	-	masculine
ז"ר	-	masculine plural
ז, נ	-	masculine, feminine
נ	-	feminine
נ"ר	-	feminine plural

BASIC CONCEPTS

Basic concepts. Part 1

1. Pronouns

I, me	ani	אֲנִי (ז, נ)
you (masc.)	ata	אַתָּה (ז)
you (fem.)	at	אַתְּ (נ)
he	hu	הוּא (ז)
she	hi	הִיא (נ)
we	a'naxnu	אֲנַחְנוּ (ז, נ)
you (masc.)	atem	אַתֶּם (ז"ר)
you (fem.)	aten	אַתֶּן (נ"ר)
you (polite, sing.)	ata, at	אַתָּה (ז), אַתְּ (נ)
you (polite, pl)	atem, aten	אַתֶּם (ז"ר), אַתֶּן (נ"ר)
they (masc.)	hem	הֵם (ז"ר)
they (fem.)	hen	הֵן (נ"ר)

2. Greetings. Salutations. Farewells

Hello! (fam.)	ʃalom!	שָׁלוֹם!
Hello! (form.)	ʃalom!	שָׁלוֹם!
Good morning!	'boker tov!	בּוֹקֶר טוֹב!
Good afternoon!	tsaha'rayim tovim!	צָהֳרַיִים טוֹבִים!
Good evening!	'erev tov!	עֶרֶב טוֹב!
to say hello	lomar ʃalom	לוֹמַר שָׁלוֹם
Hi! (hello)	hai!	הַיי!
greeting (n)	ahlan	אַהְלָן
to greet (vt)	lomar ʃalom	לוֹמַר שָׁלוֹם
How are you? (form.)	ma ʃlomeχ?, ma ʃlomχa?	מַה שְׁלוֹמְךָ? (ז), מַה שְׁלוֹמֵךְ?(נ)
How are you? (fam.)	ma niʃma?	מַה נִשְׁמָע?
What's new?	ma χadaʃ?	מַה חָדָשׁ?
Bye-Bye! Goodbye!	lehitra'ot!	לְהִתְרָאוֹת!
Bye!	bai!	בַּיי!
See you soon!	lehitra'ot bekarov!	לְהִתְרָאוֹת בְּקָרוֹב!
Farewell!	heye ʃalom!	הֱיֵה שָׁלוֹם!
Farewell! (form.)	lehitra'ot!	לְהִתְרָאוֹת!
to say goodbye	lomar lehitra'ot	לוֹמַר לְהִתְרָאוֹת

So long!	bai!	ביי!
Thank you!	toda!	תודה!
Thank you very much!	toda raba!	תודה רבה!
You're welcome	bevakaʃa	בְּבַקָשָׁה
Don't mention it!	al lo davar	עַל לֹא דָבָר
It was nothing	ein be'ad ma	אֵין בְּעַד מָה
Excuse me!	sliχa!	סליחה!
to excuse (forgive)	lis'loaχ	לסלוח
to apologize (vi)	lehitnatsel	להתנצל
My apologies	ani mitnatsel,	אֲנִי מִתְנַצֵּל (ז),
	ani mitna'tselet	אֲנִי מִתְנַצֶּלֶת (נ)
I'm sorry!	ani mitsta'er,	אֲנִי מִצְטַעֵר (ז),
	ani mitsta''eret	אֲנִי מִצְטַעֶרֶת (נ)
to forgive (vt)	lis'loaχ	לסלוח
It's okay! (that's all right)	lo nora	לא נורא
please (adv)	bevakaʃa	בְּבַקָשָׁה
Don't forget!	al tiʃkaχ!	אַל תִּשְׁכַּח! (ז)
Certainly!	'betaχ!	בֶּטַח!
Of course not!	'betaχ ʃelo!	בֶּטַח שֶׁלֹא!
Okay! (I agree)	okei!	אוֹקֵיי!
That's enough!	maspik!	מַסְפִּיק!

3. How to address

Excuse me, ...	sliχa!	סליחה!
mister, sir	adon	אָדוֹן
ma'am	gvirti	גְבִרְתִּי
miss	'gveret	גְבֶרֶת
young man	baχur tsa'ir	בָּחוּר צָעִיר
young man (little boy, kid)	'yeled	יֶלֶד
miss (little girl)	yalda	יַלְדָה

4. Cardinal numbers. Part 1

0 zero	'efes	אֶפֶס (ז)
1 one	eχad	אֶחָד (ז)
1 one (fem.)	aχat	אַחַת (נ)
2 two	'ʃtayim	שְׁתַיִים (נ)
3 three	ʃaloʃ	שָׁלוֹש (נ)
4 four	arba	אַרְבַּע (נ)
5 five	χameʃ	חָמֵש (נ)
6 six	ʃeʃ	שֵׁש (נ)
7 seven	'ʃeva	שֶׁבַע (נ)
8 eight	'ʃmone	שְׁמוֹנֶה (נ)

9 nine	'teʃa	תֵּשַׁע (נ)
10 ten	'eser	עֶשֶׂר (נ)
11 eleven	aχat esre	אַחַת־עֶשְׂרֵה (נ)
12 twelve	ʃteim esre	שְׁתֵּים־עֶשְׂרֵה (נ)
13 thirteen	ʃloʃ esre	שְׁלוֹשׁ־עֶשְׂרֵה (נ)
14 fourteen	arba esre	אַרְבַּע־עֶשְׂרֵה (נ)
15 fifteen	χameʃ esre	חֲמֵשׁ־עֶשְׂרֵה (נ)
16 sixteen	ʃeʃ esre	שֵׁשׁ־עֶשְׂרֵה (נ)
17 seventeen	ʃva esre	שְׁבַע־עֶשְׂרֵה (נ)
18 eighteen	ʃmone esre	שְׁמוֹנֶה־עֶשְׂרֵה (נ)
19 nineteen	tʃa esre	תְּשַׁע־עֶשְׂרֵה (נ)
20 twenty	esrim	עֶשְׂרִים
21 twenty-one	esrim ve'eχad	עֶשְׂרִים וְאֶחָד
22 twenty-two	esrim u'ʃnayim	עֶשְׂרִים וּשְׁנַיִים
23 twenty-three	esrim uʃloʃa	עֶשְׂרִים וּשְׁלוֹשָׁה
30 thirty	ʃloʃim	שְׁלוֹשִׁים
31 thirty-one	ʃloʃim ve'eχad	שְׁלוֹשִׁים וְאֶחָד
32 thirty-two	ʃloʃim u'ʃnayim	שְׁלוֹשִׁים וּשְׁנַיִים
33 thirty-three	ʃloʃim uʃloʃa	שְׁלוֹשִׁים וּשְׁלוֹשָׁה
40 forty	arbaʿim	אַרְבָּעִים
41 forty-one	arbaʿim ve'eχad	אַרְבָּעִים וְאֶחָד
42 forty-two	arbaʿim u'ʃnayim	אַרְבָּעִים וּשְׁנַיִים
43 forty-three	arbaʿim uʃloʃa	אַרְבָּעִים וּשְׁלוֹשָׁה
50 fifty	χamiʃim	חֲמִישִׁים
51 fifty-one	χamiʃim ve'eχad	חֲמִישִׁים וְאֶחָד
52 fifty-two	χamiʃim u'ʃnayim	חֲמִישִׁים וּשְׁנַיִים
53 fifty-three	χamiʃim uʃloʃa	חֲמִישִׁים וּשְׁלוֹשָׁה
60 sixty	ʃiʃim	שִׁישִׁים
61 sixty-one	ʃiʃim ve'eχad	שִׁישִׁים וְאֶחָד
62 sixty-two	ʃiʃim u'ʃnayim	שִׁישִׁים וּשְׁנַיִים
63 sixty-three	ʃiʃim uʃloʃa	שִׁישִׁים וּשְׁלוֹשָׁה
70 seventy	ʃivʿim	שִׁבְעִים
71 seventy-one	ʃivʿim ve'eχad	שִׁבְעִים וְאֶחָד
72 seventy-two	ʃivʿim u'ʃnayim	שִׁבְעִים וּשְׁנַיִים
73 seventy-three	ʃivʿim uʃloʃa	שִׁבְעִים וּשְׁלוֹשָׁה
80 eighty	ʃmonim	שְׁמוֹנִים
81 eighty-one	ʃmonim ve'eχad	שְׁמוֹנִים וְאֶחָד
82 eighty-two	ʃmonim u'ʃnayim	שְׁמוֹנִים וּשְׁנַיִים
83 eighty-three	ʃmonim uʃloʃa	שְׁמוֹנִים וּשְׁלוֹשָׁה
90 ninety	tiʃim	תִּשְׁעִים
91 ninety-one	tiʃim ve'eχad	תִּשְׁעִים וְאֶחָד
92 ninety-two	tiʃim u'ʃayim	תִּשְׁעִים וּשְׁנַיִים
93 ninety-three	tiʃim uʃloʃa	תִּשְׁעִים וּשְׁלוֹשָׁה

5. Cardinal numbers. Part 2

100 one hundred	'me'a	מֵאָה (נ)
200 two hundred	ma'tayim	מָאתַיִם
300 three hundred	ʃloʃ me'ot	שְׁלוֹשׁ מֵאוֹת (נ)
400 four hundred	arba me'ot	אַרְבַּע מֵאוֹת (נ)
500 five hundred	xameʃ me'ot	חָמֵשׁ מֵאוֹת (נ)
600 six hundred	ʃeʃ me'ot	שֵׁשׁ מֵאוֹת (נ)
700 seven hundred	ʃva me'ot	שְׁבַע מֵאוֹת (נ)
800 eight hundred	ʃmone me'ot	שְׁמוֹנֶה מֵאוֹת (נ)
900 nine hundred	tʃa me'ot	תְּשַׁע מֵאוֹת (נ)
1000 one thousand	'elef	אֶלֶף (ז)
2000 two thousand	al'payim	אַלְפַּיִם (ז)
3000 three thousand	'ʃloʃet alafim	שְׁלוֹשֶׁת אֲלָפִים (ז)
10000 ten thousand	a'seret alafim	עֲשֶׂרֶת אֲלָפִים (ז)
one hundred thousand	'me'a 'elef	מֵאָה אֶלֶף (ז)
million	milyon	מִילְיוֹן (ז)
billion	milyard	מִילְיַארְד (ז)

6. Ordinal numbers

first (adj)	riʃon	רִאשׁוֹן
second (adj)	ʃeni	שֵׁנִי
third (adj)	ʃliʃi	שְׁלִישִׁי
fourth (adj)	revi'i	רְבִיעִי
fifth (adj)	xamiʃi	חֲמִישִׁי
sixth (adj)	ʃiʃi	שִׁישִׁי
seventh (adj)	ʃvi'i	שְׁבִיעִי
eighth (adj)	ʃmini	שְׁמִינִי
ninth (adj)	tʃi'i	תְּשִׁיעִי
tenth (adj)	asiri	עֲשִׂירִי

7. Numbers. Fractions

fraction	'ʃever	שֶׁבֶר (ז)
one half	'xetsi	חֲצִי (ז)
one third	ʃliʃ	שְׁלִישׁ (ז)
one quarter	'reva	רֶבַע (ז)
one eighth	ʃminit	שְׁמִינִית (נ)
one tenth	asirit	עֲשִׂירִית (נ)
two thirds	ʃnei ʃliʃim	שְׁנֵי שְׁלִישִׁים (ז)
three quarters	'ʃloʃet riv'ei	שְׁלוֹשֶׁת רְבָעֵי

8. Numbers. Basic operations

subtraction	xisur	חִיסוּר (ז)
to subtract (vi, vt)	lexaser	לְחַסֵר
division	xiluk	חִילוּק (ז)
to divide (vt)	lexalek	לְחַלֵק
addition	xibur	חִיבּוּר (ז)
to add up (vt)	lexaber	לְחַבֵּר
to add (vi, vt)	lexaber	לְחַבֵּר
multiplication	'kefel	כֶּפֶל (ז)
to multiply (vt)	lehaxpil	לְהַכְפִּיל

9. Numbers. Miscellaneous

digit, figure	sifra	סִפְרָה (נ)
number	mispar	מִסְפָּר (ז)
numeral	ʃem mispar	שֵׁם מִסְפָּר (ז)
minus sign	'minus	מִינוּס (ז)
plus sign	plus	פְּלוּס (ז)
formula	nusxa	נוּסְחָה (נ)
calculation	xiʃuv	חִישׁוּב (ז)
to count (vi, vt)	lispor	לִסְפּוֹר
to count up	lexaʃev	לְחַשֵׁב
to compare (vt)	lehaʃvot	לְהַשְׁווֹת
How much?	'kama?	כַּמָה?
How many?	'kama?	כַּמָה?
sum, total	sxum	סְכוּם (ז)
result	totsa'a	תוֹצָאָה (נ)
remainder	ʃe'erit	שְׁאֵרִית (נ)
a few (e.g., ~ years ago)	'kama	כַּמָה
little (I had ~ time)	ktsat	קְצָת
few (I have ~ friends)	me'at	מְעַט
a little (~ tired)	me'at	מְעַט
the rest	ʃe'ar	שְׁאָר (ז)
one and a half	exad va'xetsi	אֶחָד וָחֵצִי (ז)
dozen	tresar	תְּרֵיסָר (ז)
in half (adv)	'xetsi 'xetsi	חֲצִי חֲצִי
equally (evenly)	ʃave beʃave	שָׁוֶה בְּשָׁוֶה
half	'xetsi	חֲצִי (ז)
time (three ~s)	'pa'am	פַּעַם (נ)

10. The most important verbs. Part 1

to advise (vt)	leya'ets	לְיַיעֵץ
to agree (say yes)	lehaskim	לְהַסכִּים
to answer (vi, vt)	la'anot	לַעֲנוֹת
to apologize (vi)	lehitnatsel	לְהִתנַצֵל
to arrive (vi)	leha'gi'a	לְהַגִיעַ
to ask (~ oneself)	liʃol	לִשאוֹל
to ask (~ sb to do sth)	levakeʃ	לְבַקֵש
to be (vi)	lihyot	לִהיוֹת
to be afraid	lefaxed	לְפַחֵד
to be hungry	lihyot ra'ev	לִהיוֹת רָעֵב
to be interested in ...	lehit'anyen be...	לְהִתעַניֵין בְּ...
to be needed	lehidareʃ	לְהִידָרֵש
to be surprised	lehitpale	לְהִתפַּלֵא
to be thirsty	lihyot tsame	לִהיוֹת צָמֵא
to begin (vt)	lehatxil	לְהַתחִיל
to belong to ...	lehiʃtayex	לְהִשתַייֵך
to boast (vi)	lehitravrev	לְהִתרַברֵב
to break (split into pieces)	liʃbor	לִשבּוֹר
to call (~ for help)	likro	לִקרוֹא
can (v aux)	yaxol	יָכוֹל
to catch (vt)	litfos	לִתפּוֹס
to change (vt)	leʃanot	לְשַנוֹת
to choose (select)	livxor	לִבחוֹר
to come down (the stairs)	la'redet	לָרֶדֶת
to compare (vt)	lehaʃvot	לְהַשווֹת
to complain (vi, vt)	lehitlonen	לְהִתלוֹנֵן
to confuse (mix up)	lehitbalbel	לְהִתבַּלבֵּל
to continue (vt)	lehamʃix	לְהַמשִיך
to control (vt)	liʃlot	לִשלוֹט
to cook (dinner)	levaʃel	לְבַשֵל
to cost (vt)	la'alot	לַעֲלוֹת
to count (add up)	lispor	לִספּוֹר
to count on ...	lismox al	לִסמוֹך עַל
to create (vt)	litsor	לִיצוֹר
to cry (weep)	livkot	לִבכּוֹת

11. The most important verbs. Part 2

to deceive (vi, vt)	leramot	לְרַמוֹת
to decorate (tree, street)	lekaʃet	לְקַשֵט
to defend (a country, etc.)	lehagen	לְהָגֵן

to demand (request firmly)	lidroʃ	לִדְרוֹשׁ
to dig (vt)	laxpor	לַחְפּוֹר
to discuss (vt)	ladun	לָדוּן
to do (vt)	la'asot	לַעֲשׂוֹת
to doubt (have doubts)	lefakpek	לְפַקְפֵּק
to drop (let fall)	lehapil	לְהַפִּיל
to enter (room, house, etc.)	lehikanes	לְהִיכָּנֵס
to excuse (forgive)	lis'loax	לִסְלוֹחַ
to exist (vi)	lehitkayem	לְהִתְקַיֵּם
to expect (foresee)	laxazot	לַחֲזוֹת
to explain (vt)	lehasbir	לְהַסְבִּיר
to fall (vi)	lipol	לִיפּוֹל
to find (vt)	limtso	לִמְצוֹא
to finish (vt)	lesayem	לְסַיֵּים
to fly (vi)	la'uf	לָעוּף
to follow ... (come after)	la'akov axarei	לַעֲקוֹב אַחֲרֵי
to forget (vi, vt)	liʃkoax	לִשְׁכּוֹחַ
to forgive (vt)	lis'loax	לִסְלוֹחַ
to give (vt)	latet	לָתֵת
to give a hint	lirmoz	לִרְמוֹז
to go (on foot)	la'lexet	לָלֶכֶת
to go for a swim	lehitraxets	לְהִתְרַחֵץ
to go out (for dinner, etc.)	latset	לָצֵאת
to guess (the answer)	lenaxeʃ	לְנַחֵשׁ
to have (vt)	lehaxzik	לְהַחֲזִיק
to have breakfast	le'exol aruxat 'boker	לֶאֱכוֹל אֲרוּחַת בּוֹקֶר
to have dinner	le'exol aruxat 'erev	לֶאֱכוֹל אֲרוּחַת עֶרֶב
to have lunch	le'exol aruxat tsaha'rayim	לֶאֱכוֹל אֲרוּחַת צָהֳרַיִים
to hear (vt)	liʃmo'a	לִשְׁמוֹעַ
to help (vt)	la'azor	לַעֲזוֹר
to hide (vt)	lehastir	לְהַסְתִּיר
to hope (vi, vt)	lekavot	לְקַוּוֹת
to hunt (vi, vt)	latsud	לָצוּד
to hurry (vi)	lemaher	לְמַהֵר

12. The most important verbs. Part 3

to inform (vt)	leho'dia	לְהוֹדִיעַ
to insist (vi, vt)	lehit'akeʃ	לְהִתְעַקֵּשׁ
to insult (vt)	leha'aliv	לְהַעֲלִיב
to invite (vt)	lehazmin	לְהַזְמִין
to joke (vi)	lehitba'deax	לְהִתְבַּדֵּחַ

to keep (vt)	lißmor	לִשְׁמוֹר
to keep silent	liʃtok	לִשְׁתוֹק
to kill (vt)	laharog	לַהֲרוֹג
to know (sb)	lehakir et	לְהַכִּיר אֶת
to know (sth)	la'da'at	לָדַעַת
to laugh (vi)	litsχok	לִצְחוֹק

to liberate (city, etc.)	leʃaχrer	לְשַׁחְרֵר
to like (I like …)	limtso χen be'ei'nayim	לִמְצוֹא חֵן בְּעֵינַיִים
to look for … (search)	leχapes	לְחַפֵּשׂ
to love (sb)	le'ehov	לֶאֱהוֹב
to make a mistake	lit'ot	לִטְעוֹת

to manage, to run	lenahel	לְנַהֵל
to mean (signify)	lomar	לוֹמַר
to mention (talk about)	lehazkir	לְהַזְכִּיר
to miss (school, etc.)	lehaχsir	לְהַחְסִיר
to notice (see)	lasim lev	לָשִׂים לֵב

to object (vi, vt)	lehitnaged	לְהִתְנַגֵּד
to observe (see)	litspot, lehaʃkif	לִצְפּוֹת, לְהַשְׁקִיף
to open (vt)	lif'toaχ	לִפְתּוֹחַ
to order (meal, etc.)	lehazmin	לְהַזְמִין
to order (mil.)	lifkod	לִפְקוֹד
to own (possess)	lihyot 'ba'al ʃel	לִהְיוֹת בַּעַל שֶׁל

to participate (vi)	lehiʃtatef	לְהִשְׁתַּתֵּף
to pay (vi, vt)	leʃalem	לְשַׁלֵּם
to permit (vt)	leharʃot	לְהַרְשׁוֹת
to plan (vt)	letaχnen	לְתַכְנֵן
to play (children)	lesaχek	לְשַׂחֵק

to pray (vi, vt)	lehitpalel	לְהִתְפַּלֵּל
to prefer (vt)	leha'adif	לְהַעֲדִיף
to promise (vt)	lehav'tiaχ	לְהַבְטִיחַ
to pronounce (vt)	levate	לְבַטֵּא
to propose (vt)	leha'tsi'a	לְהַצִּיעַ
to punish (vt)	leha'aniʃ	לְהַעֲנִישׁ

13. The most important verbs. Part 4

to read (vi, vt)	likro	לִקְרוֹא
to recommend (vt)	lehamlits	לְהַמְלִיץ
to refuse (vi, vt)	lesarev	לְסָרֵב
to regret (be sorry)	lehitsta'er	לְהִצְטַעֵר
to rent (sth from sb)	liskor	לִשְׂכּוֹר

to repeat (say again)	laχazor al	לַחֲזוֹר עַל
to reserve, to book	lehazmin meroʃ	לְהַזְמִין מֵרֹאשׁ
to run (vi)	laruts	לָרוּץ

to save (rescue)	lehatsil	לְהַצִּיל
to say (~ thank you)	lomar	לוֹמַר
to scold (vt)	linzof	לִנְזוֹף
to see (vt)	lir'ot	לִרְאוֹת
to sell (vt)	limkor	לִמְכּוֹר
to send (vt)	liʃloax	לִשְׁלוֹחַ
to shoot (vi)	lirot	לִירוֹת
to shout (vi)	lits'ok	לִצְעוֹק
to show (vt)	lehar'ot	לְהַרְאוֹת
to sign (document)	laxtom	לַחְתוֹם
to sit down (vi)	lehityaʃev	לְהִתְיַישֵׁב
to smile (vi)	lexayex	לְחַיֵּיךְ
to speak (vi, vt)	ledaber	לְדַבֵּר
to steal (money, etc.)	lignov	לִגְנוֹב
to stop (for pause, etc.)	la'atsor	לַעֲצוֹר
to stop (please ~ calling me)	lehafsik	לְהַפְסִיק
to study (vt)	lilmod	לִלְמוֹד
to swim (vi)	lisxot	לִשְׂחוֹת
to take (vt)	la'kaxat	לָקַחַת
to think (vi, vt)	laxʃov	לַחְשׁוֹב
to threaten (vt)	le'ayem	לְאַיֵּים
to touch (with hands)	la'ga'at	לָנֵעַת
to translate (vt)	letargem	לְתַרְגֵּם
to trust (vt)	liv'toax	לִבְטוֹחַ
to try (attempt)	lenasot	לְנַסוֹת
to turn (e.g., ~ left)	lifnot	לִפְנוֹת
to underestimate (vt)	leham'it be''erex	לְהַמְעִיט בְּעֵרֶךְ
to understand (vt)	lehavin	לְהָבִין
to unite (vt)	le'axed	לְאַחֵד
to wait (vt)	lehamtin	לְהַמְתִּין
to want (wish, desire)	lirtsot	לִרְצוֹת
to warn (vt)	lehazhir	לְהַזְהִיר
to work (vi)	la'avod	לַעֲבוֹד
to write (vt)	lixtov	לִכְתּוֹב
to write down	lirʃom	לִרְשׁוֹם

14. Colors

color	'tseva	צֶבַע (ז)
shade (tint)	gavan	גָּווָן (ז)
hue	gavan	גָּווָן (ז)
rainbow	'keʃet	קֶשֶׁת (נ)

white (adj)	lavan	לָבָן
black (adj)	ʃaxor	שָׁחוֹר
gray (adj)	afor	אָפוֹר
green (adj)	yarok	יָרוֹק
yellow (adj)	tsahov	צָהוֹב
red (adj)	adom	אָדוֹם
blue (adj)	kaxol	כָּחוֹל
light blue (adj)	taxol	תְכוֹל
pink (adj)	varod	וָרוֹד
orange (adj)	katom	כָּתוֹם
violet (adj)	segol	סָגוֹל
brown (adj)	xum	חוּם
golden (adj)	zahov	זָהוֹב
silvery (adj)	kasuf	כָּסוּף
beige (adj)	beʒ	בֶּז'
cream (adj)	be'tseva krem	בְּצֶבַע קרֶם
turquoise (adj)	turkiz	טוּרקִיז
cherry red (adj)	bordo	בּוֹרדוֹ
lilac (adj)	segol	סָגוֹל
crimson (adj)	patol	פָּטוֹל
light (adj)	bahir	בָּהִיר
dark (adj)	kehe	כֵּהֶה
bright, vivid (adj)	bohek	בּוֹהֵק
colored (pencils)	tsiv'oni	צִבעוֹנִי
color (e.g., ~ film)	tsiv'oni	צִבעוֹנִי
black-and-white (adj)	ʃaxor lavan	שָׁחוֹר-לָבָן
plain (one-colored)	xad tsiv'i	חַד-צִבעִי
multicolored (adj)	sasgoni	סַסגוֹנִי

15. Questions

Who?	mi?	מִי?
What?	ma?	מָה?
Where? (at, in)	'eifo?	אֵיפֹה?
Where (to)?	le'an?	לְאָן?
From where?	me''eifo?	מֵאֵיפֹה?
When?	matai?	מָתַי?
Why? (What for?)	'lama?	לָמָה?
Why? (~ are you crying?)	ma'du'a?	מַדוּעַ?
What for?	biʃvil ma?	בִּשׁבִיל מָה?
How? (in what way)	eix, keitsad?	כֵּיצַד? אֵיך?
What? (What kind of …?)	'eize?	אֵיזָה?
Which?	'eize?	אֵיזָה?

To whom?	lemi?	לְמִי?
About whom?	al mi?	עַל מִי?
About what?	al ma?	עַל מָה?
With whom?	im mi?	עִם מִי?
How many? How much?	'kama?	כַּמָה?
Whose?	ʃel mi?	שֶל מִי?

16. Prepositions

with (accompanied by)	im	עִם
without	bli, lelo	בְּלִי, לְלֹא
to (indicating direction)	le...	לְ...
about (talking ~ ...)	al	עַל
before (in time)	lifnei	לִפנֵי
in front of ...	lifnei	לִפנֵי
under (beneath, below)	mi'taxat le...	מִתַחַת לְ...
above (over)	me'al	מֵעַל
on (atop)	al	עַל
from (off, out of)	mi, me	מִ, מֵ
of (made from)	mi, me	מִ, מֵ
in (e.g., ~ ten minutes)	tox	תוֹך
over (across the top of)	'derex	דֶרֶך

17. Function words. Adverbs. Part 1

Where? (at, in)	'eifo?	אֵיפֹה?
here (adv)	po, kan	פֹּה, כָּאן
there (adv)	ʃam	שָם
somewhere (to be)	'eifo ʃehu	אֵיפֹה שֶהוּא
nowhere (not anywhere)	beʃum makom	בְּשוּם מָקוֹם
by (near, beside)	leyad ...	לְיַד ...
by the window	leyad haxalon	לְיַד הַחַלוֹן
Where (to)?	le'an?	לְאָן?
here (e.g., come ~!)	'hena, lekan	הֵנָה, לְכָאן
there (e.g., to go ~)	leʃam	לְשָם
from here (adv)	mikan	מִכָּאן
from there (adv)	miʃam	מִשָם
close (adv)	karov	קָרוֹב
far (adv)	raxok	רָחוֹק
near (e.g., ~ Paris)	leyad	לְיַד
nearby (adv)	karov	קָרוֹב

not far (adv)	lo raxok	לֹא רָחוֹק
left (adj)	smali	שְׂמָאלִי
on the left	mismol	מִשְּׂמֹאל
to the left	'smola	שְׂמֹאלָה
right (adj)	yemani	יְמָנִי
on the right	miyamin	מִיָּמִין
to the right	ya'mina	יָמִינָה
in front (adv)	mika'dima	מִקָּדִימָה
front (as adj)	kidmi	קִדְמִי
ahead (the kids ran ~)	ka'dima	קָדִימָה
behind (adv)	me'axor	מֵאָחוֹר
from behind	me'axor	מֵאָחוֹר
back (towards the rear)	a'xora	אֲחוֹרָה
middle	'emtsa	אֶמְצַע (ז)
in the middle	ba''emtsa	בָּאֶמְצַע
at the side	mehatsad	מֵהַצַּד
everywhere (adv)	bexol makom	בְּכָל מָקוֹם
around (in all directions)	misaviv	מִסָּבִיב
from inside	mibifnim	מִבִּפְנִים
somewhere (to go)	le'an ʃehu	לְאָן שֶׁהוּא
straight (directly)	yaʃar	יָשָׁר
back (e.g., come ~)	baxazara	בַּחֲזָרָה
from anywhere	me'ei ʃam	מֵאֵי שָׁם
from somewhere	me'ei ʃam	מֵאֵי שָׁם
firstly (adv)	reʃit	רֵאשִׁית
secondly (adv)	ʃenit	שֵׁנִית
thirdly (adv)	ʃliʃit	שְׁלִישִׁית
suddenly (adv)	pit'om	פִּתְאוֹם
at first (in the beginning)	behatslaxa	בַּהַתְחָלָה
for the first time	lariʃona	לָרִאשׁוֹנָה
long before ...	zman rav lifnei ...	זְמַן רַב לִפְנֵי ...
anew (over again)	mexadaʃ	מֵחָדָשׁ
for good (adv)	letamid	לְתָמִיד
never (adv)	af 'pa'am, me'olam	מֵעוֹלָם, אַף פַּעַם
again (adv)	ʃuv	שׁוּב
now (adv)	axʃav, ka'et	עַכְשָׁיו, כָּעֵת
often (adv)	le'itim krovot	לְעִיתִּים קְרוֹבוֹת
then (adv)	az	אָז
urgently (quickly)	bidxifut	בִּדְחִיפוּת
usually (adv)	be'derex klal	בְּדֶרֶךְ כְּלָל
by the way, ...	'derex 'agav	דֶּרֶךְ אַגַּב
possible (that is ~)	efʃari	אֶפְשָׁרִי

probably (adv)	kanir'e	כַּנִּרְאֶה
maybe (adv)	ulai	אוּלַי
besides ...	xuts mize ...	חוּץ מִזֶּה ...
that's why ...	laxen	לָכֵן
in spite of ...	lamrot ...	לַמְרוֹת ...
thanks to ...	hodot le...	הוֹדוֹת ל...
what (pron.)	ma	מָה
that (conj.)	ʃe	שֶׁ
something	'maʃehu	מַשֶּׁהוּ
anything (something)	'maʃehu	מַשֶּׁהוּ
nothing	klum	כְּלוּם
who (pron.)	mi	מִי
someone	'miʃehu, 'miʃehi	מִישֶׁהוּ (ז), מִישֶׁהִי (נ)
somebody	'miʃehu, 'miʃehi	מִישֶׁהוּ (ז), מִישֶׁהִי (נ)
nobody	af exad, af axat	אַף אֶחָד (ז), אַף אַחַת (נ)
nowhere (a voyage to ~)	leʃum makom	לְשׁוּם מָקוֹם
nobody's	lo ʃayax le'af exad	לֹא שַׁיָּךְ לְאַף אֶחָד
somebody's	ʃel 'miʃehu	שֶׁל מִישֶׁהוּ
so (I'm ~ glad)	kol kax	כָּל־כָּךְ
also (as well)	gam	גַּם
too (as well)	gam	גַּם

18. Function words. Adverbs. Part 2

Why?	ma'du'a?	מַדּוּעַ?
for some reason	miʃum ma	מִשּׁוּם־מָה
because ...	miʃum ʃe	מִשּׁוּם שֶׁ
for some purpose	lematara 'kolʃehi	לְמַטָּרָה כָּלְשֶׁהִי
and	ve ...	וְ ...
or	o	אוֹ
but	aval, ulam	אֲבָל, אוּלָם
for (e.g., ~ me)	biʃvil	בִּשְׁבִיל
too (~ many people)	yoter midai	יוֹתֵר מִדַּי
only (exclusively)	rak	רַק
exactly (adv)	bediyuk	בְּדִיּוּק
about (more or less)	be''erex	בְּעֵרֶךְ
approximately (adv)	be''erex	בְּעֵרֶךְ
approximate (adj)	meʃo'ar	מְשׁוֹעָר
almost (adv)	kim'at	כִּמְעַט
the rest	ʃe'ar	שְׁאָר (ז)
the other (second)	axer	אַחֵר
other (different)	axer	אַחֵר

each (adj)	kol	כֹּל
any (no matter which)	kolʃehu	כָּלְשֶׁהוּ
many, much (a lot of)	harbe	הַרְבֵּה
many people	harbe	הַרְבֵּה
all (everyone)	kulam	כּוּלָם
in return for …	tmurat …	תמורת …
in exchange (adv)	bitmura	בִּתְמוּרָה
by hand (made)	bayad	בַּיָד
hardly (negative opinion)	safek im	סָפֵק אִם
probably (adv)	karov levadai	קָרוֹב לְוַודַאי
on purpose (intentionally)	'davka	דַווקָא
by accident (adv)	bemikre	בְּמִקְרֶה
very (adv)	me'od	מְאוֹד
for example (adv)	lemaʃal	לְמָשָׁל
between	bein	בֵּין
among	be'kerev	בְּקֶרֶב
so much (such a lot)	kol kaχ harbe	כָּל־כָּךְ הַרְבֵּה
especially (adv)	bimyuχad	בְּמִיוּחָד

Basic concepts. Part 2

19. Weekdays

Monday	yom ʃeni	יוֹם שֵׁנִי (ז)
Tuesday	yom ʃliʃi	יוֹם שְׁלִישִׁי (ז)
Wednesday	yom revi'i	יוֹם רְבִיעִי (ז)
Thursday	yom xamiʃi	יוֹם חֲמִישִׁי (ז)
Friday	yom ʃiʃi	יוֹם שִׁישִׁי (ז)
Saturday	ʃabat	שַׁבָּת (נ)
Sunday	yom riʃon	יוֹם רִאשׁוֹן (ז)

today (adv)	hayom	הַיוֹם
tomorrow (adv)	maxar	מָחָר
the day after tomorrow	maxara'tayim	מָחֳרָתַיִים
yesterday (adv)	etmol	אֶתמוֹל
the day before yesterday	ʃilʃom	שִׁלשׁוֹם

day	yom	יוֹם (ז)
working day	yom avoda	יוֹם עֲבוֹדָה (ז)
public holiday	yom xag	יוֹם חַג (ז)
day off	yom menuxa	יוֹם מְנוּחָה (ז)
weekend	sof ʃa'vu'a	סוֹף שָׁבוּעַ

all day long	kol hayom	כָּל הַיוֹם
the next day (adv)	lamaxarat	לַמָחֳרָת
two days ago	lifnei yo'mayim	לִפנֵי יוֹמַיִים
the day before	'erev	עֶרֶב
daily (adj)	yomyomi	יוֹמיוֹמִי
every day (adv)	midei yom	מִדֵי יוֹם

week	ʃa'vua	שָׁבוּעַ (ז)
last week (adv)	baʃa'vu'a ʃe'avar	בַּשָׁבוּעַ שֶׁעָבַר
next week (adv)	baʃa'vu'a haba	בַּשָׁבוּעַ הַבָּא
weekly (adj)	ʃvu'i	שְׁבוּעִי
every week (adv)	kol ʃa'vu'a	כָּל שָׁבוּעַ
twice a week	pa'a'mayim beʃa'vu'a	פַּעֲמַיִים בְּשָׁבוּעַ
every Tuesday	kol yom ʃliʃi	כָּל יוֹם שְׁלִישִׁי

20. Hours. Day and night

morning	'boker	בּוֹקֶר (ז)
in the morning	ba'boker	בַּבּוֹקֶר
noon, midday	tsaha'rayim	צָהֳרַיִים (ז״ר)

in the afternoon	aχar hatsaha'rayim	אַחַר הַצָהֳרַיִים
evening	'erev	עֶרֶב (ז)
in the evening	ba''erev	בָּעֶרֶב
night	'laila	לַיְלָה (ז)
at night	ba'laila	בַּלַיְלָה
midnight	χatsot	חֲצוֹת (נ)
second	ʃniya	שְׁנִיָּה (נ)
minute	daka	דַקָה (נ)
hour	ʃa'a	שָׁעָה (נ)
half an hour	χatsi ʃa'a	חֲצִי שָׁעָה (נ)
a quarter-hour	'reva ʃa'a	רֶבַע שָׁעָה (ז)
fifteen minutes	χameʃ esre dakot	חֲמֵשׁ עֶשְׂרֵה דַקוֹת
24 hours	yemama	יְמָמָה (נ)
sunrise	zriχa	זְרִיחָה (נ)
dawn	'ʃaχar	שַׁחַר (ז)
early morning	'ʃaχar	שַׁחַר (ז)
sunset	ʃki'a	שְׁקִיעָה (נ)
early in the morning	mukdam ba'boker	מוּקְדָם בַּבּוֹקֶר
this morning	ha'boker	הַבּוֹקֶר
tomorrow morning	maχar ba'boker	מָחָר בַּבּוֹקֶר
this afternoon	hayom aχarei hatzaha'rayim	הַיוֹם אַחֲרֵי הַצָהֳרַיִים
in the afternoon	aχar hatsaha'rayim	אַחַר הַצָהֳרַיִים
tomorrow afternoon	maχar aχarei hatsaha'rayim	מָחָר אַחֲרֵי הַצָהֳרַיִים
tonight (this evening)	ha''erev	הָעֶרֶב
tomorrow night	maχar ba''erev	מָחָר בָּעֶרֶב
at 3 o'clock sharp	baʃa'a ʃaloʃ bediyuk	בְּשָׁעָה שָׁלוֹשׁ בְּדִיוּק
about 4 o'clock	bisvivot arba	בִּסְבִיבוֹת אַרְבַּע
by 12 o'clock	ad ʃteim esre	עַד שְׁתֵּים-עֶשְׂרֵה
in 20 minutes	be'od esrim dakot	בְּעוֹד עֶשְׂרִים דַקוֹת
in an hour	be'od ʃa'a	בְּעוֹד שָׁעָה
on time (adv)	bazman	בַּזְמַן
a quarter of ...	'reva le...	רֶבַע לְ...
within an hour	toχ ʃa'a	תוֹךְ שָׁעָה
every 15 minutes	kol 'reva ʃa'a	כָּל רֶבַע שָׁעָה
round the clock	misaviv laʃa'on	מִסָבִיב לַשָׁעוֹן

21. Months. Seasons

January	'yanu'ar	יָנוּאָר (ז)
February	'febru'ar	פֶבְּרוּאָר (ז)

March	merts	מֶרְץ (ז)
April	april	אַפְּרִיל (ז)
May	mai	מַאי (ז)
June	'yuni	יוּנִי (ז)
July	'yuli	יוּלִי (ז)
August	'ogust	אוֹגוּסְט (ז)
September	sep'tember	סֶפְּטֶמְבֶּר (ז)
October	ok'tober	אוֹקְטוֹבֶּר (ז)
November	no'vember	נוֹבֶמְבֶּר (ז)
December	de'tsember	דֶּצֶמְבֶּר (ז)
spring	aviv	אָבִיב (ז)
in spring	ba'aviv	בָּאָבִיב
spring (as adj)	avivi	אֲבִיבִי
summer	'kayits	קַיִץ (ז)
in summer	ba'kayits	בַּקַיִץ
summer (as adj)	ketsi	קֵיצִי
fall	stav	סְתָיו (ז)
in fall	bestav	בִּסְתָיו
fall (as adj)	stavi	סְתָווִי
winter	'xoref	חוֹרֶף (ז)
in winter	ba'xoref	בַּחוֹרֶף
winter (as adj)	xorpi	חוֹרְפִּי
month	'xodeʃ	חוֹדֶשׁ (ז)
this month	ha'xodeʃ	הַחוֹדֶשׁ
next month	ba'xodeʃ haba	בַּחוֹדֶשׁ הַבָּא
last month	ba'xodeʃ ʃe'avar	בַּחוֹדֶשׁ שֶׁעָבַר
a month ago	lifnei 'xodeʃ	לִפְנֵי חוֹדֶשׁ
in a month (a month later)	be'od 'xodeʃ	בְּעוֹד חוֹדֶשׁ
in 2 months (2 months later)	be'od xod'ʃayim	בְּעוֹד חוֹדְשַׁיִים
the whole month	kol ha'xodeʃ	כָּל הַחוֹדֶשׁ
all month long	kol ha'xodeʃ	כָּל הַחוֹדֶשׁ
monthly (~ magazine)	xodʃi	חוֹדְשִׁי
monthly (adv)	xodʃit	חוֹדְשִׁית
every month	kol 'xodeʃ	כָּל חוֹדֶשׁ
twice a month	pa'a'mayim be'xodeʃ	פַּעֲמַיִים בְּחוֹדֶשׁ
year	ʃana	שָׁנָה (נ)
this year	haʃana	הַשָׁנָה
next year	baʃana haba'a	בַּשָׁנָה הַבָּאָה
last year	baʃana ʃe'avra	בַּשָׁנָה שֶׁעָבְרָה
a year ago	lifnei ʃana	לִפְנֵי שָׁנָה
in a year	be'od ʃana	בְּעוֹד שָׁנָה

in two years	be'od ʃna'tayim	בְּעוֹד שְׁנָתַיִים
the whole year	kol haʃana	כָּל הַשָׁנָה
all year long	kol haʃana	כָּל הַשָׁנָה

every year	kol ʃana	כָּל שָׁנָה
annual (adj)	ʃnati	שְׁנָתִי
annually (adv)	midei ʃana	מִדֵי שָׁנָה
4 times a year	arba pa'amim be'xodeʃ	אַרְבַּע פְּעָמִים בְּחוֹדֶשׁ

date (e.g., today's ~)	ta'arix	תַאֲרִיךְ (ז)
date (e.g., ~ of birth)	ta'arix	תַאֲרִיךְ (ז)
calendar	'luax ʃana	לוּחַ שָׁנָה (ז)

half a year	xatsi ʃana	חֲצִי שָׁנָה (ז)
six months	ʃiʃa xodaʃim, xatsi ʃana	חֲצִי שָׁנָה, שִׁישָׁה חוֹדָשִים
season (summer, etc.)	ona	עוֹנָה (נ)
century	'me'a	מֵאָה (נ)

22. Units of measurement

weight	miʃkal	מִשְקָל (ז)
length	'orex	אוֹרֶךְ (ז)
width	'roxav	רוֹחַב (ז)
height	'gova	גוֹבַהּ (ז)
depth	'omek	עוֹמֶק (ז)
volume	'nefax	נֶפַח (ז)
area	'ʃetax	שֶׁטַח (ז)

gram	gram	גרָם (ז)
milligram	miligram	מִילִיגרָם (ז)
kilogram	kilogram	קִילוֹגרָם (ז)
ton	ton	טוֹן (ז)
pound	'pa'und	פָּאוּנד (ז)
ounce	'unkiya	אוֹנקִיָה (נ)

meter	'meter	מֶטֶר (ז)
millimeter	mili'meter	מִילִימֶטֶר (ז)
centimeter	senti'meter	סַנטִימֶטֶר (ז)
kilometer	kilo'meter	קִילוֹמֶטֶר (ז)
mile	mail	מַייל (ז)

inch	intʃ	אִינץ' (ז)
foot	'regel	רֶגֶל (נ)
yard	yard	יַרד (ז)

| square meter | 'meter ra'vu'a | מֶטֶר רָבוּעַ (ז) |
| hectare | hektar | הֶקטָר (ז) |

| liter | litr | לִיטר (ז) |
| degree | ma'ala | מַעֲלָה (נ) |

volt	volt	וֹלְט (ז)
ampere	amper	אַמְפֶּר (ז)
horsepower	'koax sus	כּוֹחַ סוּס (ז)
quantity	kamut	כַּמוּת (נ)
a little bit of ...	ktsat ...	קְצָת ...
half	'xetsi	חֲצִי (ז)
dozen	tresar	תְּרֵיסָר (ז)
piece (item)	yexida	יְחִידָה (נ)
size	'godel	גּוֹדֶל (ז)
scale (map ~)	kne mida	קְנֵה מִידָה (ז)
minimal (adj)	mini'mali	מִינִימָאלִי
the smallest (adj)	hakatan beyoter	הַקָּטָן בְּיוֹתֵר
medium (adj)	memutsa	מְמוּצָּע
maximal (adj)	maksi'mali	מַקְסִימָלִי
the largest (adj)	hagadol beyoter	הַגָּדוֹל בְּיוֹתֵר

23. Containers

canning jar (glass ~)	tsin'tsenet	צִנְצֶנֶת (נ)
can	paxit	פַּחִית (נ)
bucket	dli	דְּלִי (ז)
barrel	xavit	חָבִית (נ)
wash basin (e.g., plastic ~)	gigit	גִּיגִית (נ)
tank (100L water ~)	meixal	מֵיכָל (ז)
hip flask	meimiya	מֵימִיָּה (נ)
jerrycan	'dʒerikan	גֶ'רִיקָן (ז)
tank (e.g., tank car)	mexalit	מֵיכָלִית (נ)
mug	'sefel	סֵפֶל (ז)
cup (of coffee, etc.)	'sefel	סֵפֶל (ז)
saucer	taxtit	תַּחְתִּית (נ)
glass (tumbler)	kos	כּוֹס (נ)
wine glass	ga'vi'a	גָּבִיעַ (ז)
stock pot (soup pot)	sir	סִיר (ז)
bottle (~ of wine)	bakbuk	בַּקְבּוּק (ז)
neck (of the bottle, etc.)	tsavar habakbuk	צַוָּאר הַבַּקְבּוּק (ז)
carafe (decanter)	kad	כַּד (ז)
pitcher	kankan	קַנְקַן (ז)
vessel (container)	kli	כְּלִי (ז)
pot (crock, stoneware ~)	sir 'xeres	סִיר חֶרֶס (ז)
vase	agartal	אֲגַרְטָל (ז)
bottle (perfume ~)	tsloxit	צְלוֹחִית (נ)
vial, small bottle	bakbukon	בַּקְבּוּקוֹן (ז)

tube (of toothpaste)	ʃfo'feret	שְׁפוֹפֶרֶת (נ)
sack (bag)	sak	שַׂק (ז)
bag (paper ~, plastic ~)	sakit	שַׂקִית (נ)
pack (of cigarettes, etc.)	xafisa	חֲפִיסָה (נ)

box (e.g., shoebox)	kufsa	קוּפְסָה (נ)
crate	argaz	אַרְגָּז (ז)
basket	sal	סַל (ז)

HUMAN BEING

Human being. The body

24. Head

head	roʃ	רֹאש (ז)
face	panim	פָּנִים (ז״ר)
nose	af	אַף (ז)
mouth	pe	פֶּה (ז)
eye	'ayin	עַיִן (נ)
eyes	ei'nayim	עֵינַיִים (נ״ר)
pupil	iʃon	אִישׁוֹן (ז)
eyebrow	gaba	גַבָּה (נ)
eyelash	ris	רִיס (ז)
eyelid	af'af	עַפעַף (ז)
tongue	laʃon	לָשׁוֹן (נ)
tooth	ʃen	שֵׁן (נ)
lips	sfa'tayim	שׂפָתַיִים (נ״ר)
cheekbones	atsamot leχa'yayim	עַצמוֹת לְחָיַיִם (נ״ר)
gum	χani'χayim	חָנִיכַיִים (ז״ר)
palate	χeχ	חֵך (ז)
nostrils	neχi'rayim	נְחִיכַיִים (ז״ר)
chin	santer	סַנטֵר (ז)
jaw	'leset	לֶסֶת (נ)
cheek	'leχi	לֶחִי (נ)
forehead	'metsaχ	מֵצַח (ז)
temple	raka	רַקָה (נ)
ear	'ozen	אוֹזֶן (נ)
back of the head	'oref	עוֹרֶף (ז)
neck	tsavar	צַוָואר (ז)
throat	garon	גָרוֹן (ז)
hair	se'ar	שֵׂיעָר (ז)
hairstyle	tis'roket	תִסרוֹקֶת (נ)
haircut	tis'poret	תִספּוֹרֶת (נ)
wig	pe'a	פֵּאָה (נ)
mustache	safam	שָׂפָם (ז)
beard	zakan	זָקָן (ז)
to have (a beard, etc.)	legadel	לְגַדֵל

braid	tsama	צַמָּה (נ)
sideburns	pe'ot leχa'yayim	פֵּאוֹת לְחָיַיִם (נ״ר)
red-haired (adj)	'dʒindʒi	גִ׳ינגִ׳י
gray (hair)	kasuf	כָּסוּף
bald (adj)	ke'reaχ	קֵירֵחַ
bald patch	ka'raχat	קָרַחַת (נ)
ponytail	'kuku	קוּקוּ (ז)
bangs	'poni	פּוֹנִי (ז)

25. Human body

hand	kaf yad	כַּף יָד (נ)
arm	yad	יָד (נ)
finger	'etsba	אֶצבַּע (נ)
toe	'bohen	בּוֹהֶן (נ)
thumb	agudal	אֲגוּדָל (ז)
little finger	'zeret	זֶרֶת (נ)
nail	tsi'poren	צִיפּוֹרֶן (נ)
fist	egrof	אֶגרוֹף (ז)
palm	kaf yad	כַּף יָד (נ)
wrist	ʃoreʃ kaf hayad	שׁוֹרֶשׁ כַּף הַיָד (ז)
forearm	ama	אַמָּה (נ)
elbow	marpek	מַרפֵּק (ז)
shoulder	katef	כָּתֵף (נ)
leg	'regel	רֶגֶל (נ)
foot	kaf 'regel	כַּף רֶגֶל (נ)
knee	'bereχ	בֶּרֶך (נ)
calf (part of leg)	ʃok	שׁוֹק (נ)
hip	yareχ	יָרֵך (ז)
heel	akev	עָקֵב (ז)
body	guf	גוּף (ז)
stomach	'beten	בֶּטֶן (נ)
chest	χaze	חָזֶה (ז)
breast	ʃad	שַׁד (ז)
flank	tsad	צַד (ז)
back	gav	גַב (ז)
lower back	mot'nayim	מוֹתנַיִים (ז״ר)
waist	'talya	טַליָה (נ)
navel (belly button)	tabur	טַבּוּר (ז)
buttocks	aχo'rayim	אֲחוֹרַיִים (ז״ר)
bottom	yaʃvan	יַשׁבָן (ז)
beauty mark	nekudat χen	נְקוּדַת חֵן (נ)
birthmark (café au lait spot)	'ketem leida	כֶּתֶם לֵידָה (ז)

| tattoo | kaʻaʻkuʻa | קָעֲקוּעַ (ז) |
| scar | tsaʻleket | צַלֶקֶת (נ) |

Clothing & Accessories

26. Outerwear. Coats

clothes	bgadim	בְּגָדִים (ז"ר)
outerwear	levuʃ elyon	לְבוּשׁ עֶלְיוֹן (ז)
winter clothing	bigdei 'χoref	בִּגְדֵי חוֹרֶף (ז"ר)
coat (overcoat)	me'il	מְעִיל (ז)
fur coat	me'il parva	מְעִיל פַּרְוָה (ז)
fur jacket	me'il parva katsar	מְעִיל פַּרְוָה קָצָר (ז)
down coat	me'il puχ	מְעִיל פּוּךְ (ז)
jacket (e.g., leather ~)	me'il katsar	מְעִיל קָצָר (ז)
raincoat (trenchcoat, etc.)	me'il 'geʃem	מְעִיל גֶשֶׁם (ז)
waterproof (adj)	amid be'mayim	עָמִיד בְּמַיִם

27. Men's & women's clothing

shirt (button shirt)	χultsa	חוּלצָה (נ)
pants	miχna'sayim	מִכְנָסַיִים (ז"ר)
jeans	miχnesei 'dʒins	מִכְנְסֵי ג'ינְס (ז"ר)
suit jacket	ʒaket	ז'קֵט (ז)
suit	χalifa	חֲלִיפָה (נ)
dress (frock)	simla	שִׂמלָה (נ)
skirt	χatsa'it	חֲצָאִית (נ)
blouse	χultsa	חוּלצָה (נ)
knitted jacket (cardigan, etc.)	ʒaket 'tsemer	ז'קֵט צֶמֶר (ז)
jacket (of woman's suit)	ʒaket	ז'קֵט (ז)
T-shirt	ti ʃert	טִי שֶׁרט (ז)
shorts (short trousers)	miχna'sayim ktsarim	מִכְנָסַיִים קְצָרִים (ז"ר)
tracksuit	'trening	טרֶנִינג (ז)
bathrobe	χaluk raχatsa	חָלוּק רַחצָה (ז)
pajamas	pi'dʒama	פִּיגָ'מָה (נ)
sweater	'sveder	סוֶודֶר (ז)
pullover	afuda	אֲפוּדָה (נ)
vest	vest	וֶסט (ז)
tailcoat	frak	פרָאק (ז)
tuxedo	tuk'sido	טוֹקסִידוֹ (ז)

uniform	madim	מַדִּים (ז״ר)
workwear	bigdei avoda	בִּגְדֵי עֲבוֹדָה (ז״ר)
overalls	sarbal	סַרְבָּל (ז)
coat (e.g., doctor's smock)	xaluk	חָלוּק (ז)

28. Clothing. Underwear

underwear	levanim	לְבָנִים (ז״ר)
boxers, briefs	taxtonim	תַּחְתּוֹנִים (ז״ר)
panties	taxtonim	תַּחְתּוֹנִים (ז״ר)
undershirt (A-shirt)	gufiya	גּוּפִיָּה (נ)
socks	gar'bayim	גַּרְבַּיִם (ז״ר)
nightgown	'ktonet 'laila	כּתוֹנֶת לַיְלָה (נ)
bra	xaziya	חֲזִיָּה (נ)
knee highs (knee-high socks)	birkon	בִּרְכּוֹן (ז)
pantyhose	garbonim	גַּרְבּוֹנִים (ז״ר)
stockings (thigh highs)	garbei 'nailon	גַּרְבֵּי נַיילוֹן (ז״ר)
bathing suit	'beged yam	בֶּגֶד יָם (ז)

29. Headwear

hat	'kova	כּוֹבַע (ז)
fedora	'kova 'leved	כּוֹבַע לֶבֶד (ז)
baseball cap	'kova 'beisbol	כּוֹבַע בֵּייסְבּוֹל (ז)
flatcap	'kova mitsxiya	כּוֹבַע מִצְחִיָּה (ז)
beret	baret	בֶּרֶט (ז)
hood	bardas	בַּרְדָּס (ז)
panama hat	'kova 'tembel	כּוֹבַע טֶמְבֶּל (ז)
knit cap (knitted hat)	'kova 'gerev	כּוֹבַע גֶּרֶב (ז)
headscarf	mit'paxat	מִטְפַּחַת (נ)
women's hat	'kova	כּוֹבַע (ז)
hard hat	kasda	קַסְדָּה (נ)
garrison cap	kumta	כּוּמְתָּה (נ)
helmet	kasda	קַסְדָּה (נ)
derby	mig'ba'at me'u'gelet	מִגְבַּעַת מְעוּגֶּלֶת (נ)
top hat	tsi'linder	צִילִינְדֶּר (ז)

30. Footwear

footwear	han'ala	הַנְעָלָה (נ)
shoes (men's shoes)	na'a'layim	נַעֲלַיִים (נ״ר)

shoes (women's shoes)	na'a'layim	נַעֲלַיִים (נ"ר)
boots (e.g., cowboy ~)	maga'fayim	מַגָפַיִים (נ"ר)
slippers	na'alei 'bayit	נַעֲלֵי בַּיִת (נ"ר)
tennis shoes (e.g., Nike ~)	na'alei sport	נַעֲלֵי ספורט (נ"ר)
sneakers (e.g., Converse ~)	na'alei sport	נַעֲלֵי ספורט (נ"ר)
sandals	sandalim	סַנדָלִים (ז"ר)
cobbler (shoe repairer)	sandlar	סַנדלָר (ז)
heel	akev	עָקֵב (ז)
pair (of shoes)	zug	זוּג (ז)
shoestring	sroχ	שׂרוֹך (ז)
to lace (vt)	lisroχ	לִשׂרוֹך
shoehorn	kaf na'a'layim	כַּף נַעֲלַיִים (נ)
shoe polish	miʃχat na'a'layim	מִשׁחַת נַעֲלַיִים (נ)

31. Personal accessories

gloves	kfafot	כְּפָפוֹת (נ"ר)
mittens	kfafot	כְּפָפוֹת (נ"ר)
scarf (muffler)	tsa'if	צָעִיף (ז)
glasses (eyeglasses)	miʃka'fayim	מִשׁקָפַיִים (ז"ר)
frame (eyeglass ~)	mis'geret	מִסגֶרֶת (נ)
umbrella	mitriya	מִטרִיָיה (נ)
walking stick	makel haliχa	מַקֵל הֲלִיכָה (ז)
hairbrush	miv'reʃet se'ar	מִברֶשֶׁת שֵׂיעָר (נ)
fan	menifa	מְנִיפָה (נ)
tie (necktie)	aniva	עֲנִיבָה (נ)
bow tie	anivat parpar	עֲנִיבַת פַּרפַּר (נ)
suspenders	ktefiyot	כְּתֵפִיוֹת (נ"ר)
handkerchief	mimχata	מִמחָטָה (נ)
comb	masrek	מַסרֵק (ז)
barrette	sikat roʃ	סִיכַּת רֹאשׁ (נ)
hairpin	sikat se'ar	סִיכַּת שֵׂעָר (נ)
buckle	avzam	אַבזָם (ז)
belt	χagora	חֲגוֹרָה (נ)
shoulder strap	retsu'at katef	רְצוּעַת כָּתֵף (נ)
bag (handbag)	tik	תִיק (ז)
purse	tik	תִיק (ז)
backpack	tarmil	תַרמִיל (ז)

32. Clothing. Miscellaneous

fashion	ofna	אוֹפְנָה (נ)
in vogue (adj)	ofnati	אוֹפְנָתִי
fashion designer	me'atsev ofna	מְעַצֵּב אוֹפְנָה (ז)
collar	tsavaron	צַוָּארוֹן (ז)
pocket	kis	כִּיס (ז)
pocket (as adj)	ʃel kis	שֶׁל כִּיס
sleeve	ʃarvul	שַׁרְווּל (ז)
hanging loop	mitle	מִתְלָה (ז)
fly (on trousers)	xanut	חֲנוּת (נ)
zipper (fastener)	roxsan	רוֹכְסָן (ז)
fastener	'keres	קֶרֶס (ז)
button	kaftor	כַּפְתּוֹר (ז)
buttonhole	lula'a	לוּלָאָה (נ)
to come off (ab. button)	lehitaleʃ	לְהִיתָלֵשׁ
to sew (vi, vt)	litpor	לִתְפּוֹר
to embroider (vi, vt)	lirkom	לִרְקוֹם
embroidery	rikma	רִקְמָה (נ)
sewing needle	'maxat tfira	מַחַט תְּפִירָה (נ)
thread	xut	חוּט (ז)
seam	'tefer	תֶּפֶר (ז)
to get dirty (vi)	lehitlaxlex	לְהִתְלַכְלֵךְ
stain (mark, spot)	'ketem	כֶּתֶם (ז)
to crease, crumple (vi)	lehitkamet	לְהִתְקַמֵּט
to tear, to rip (vt)	lik'ro'a	לִקְרוֹעַ
clothes moth	aʃ	עָשׁ (ז)

33. Personal care. Cosmetics

toothpaste	miʃxat ʃi'nayim	מִשְׁחַת שִׁינַיִים (נ)
toothbrush	miv'reʃet ʃi'nayim	מִבְרֶשֶׁת שִׁינַיִים (נ)
to brush one's teeth	letsax'tseax ʃi'nayim	לְצַחְצֵחַ שִׁינַיִים
razor	'ta'ar	תַּעַר (ז)
shaving cream	'ketsef gi'luax	קֶצֶף גִּילוּחַ (ז)
to shave (vi)	lehitga'leax	לְהִתְגַּלֵּחַ
soap	sabon	סַבּוֹן (ז)
shampoo	ʃampu	שַׁמְפּוּ (ז)
scissors	mispa'rayim	מִסְפָּרַיִים (ז״ר)
nail file	ptsira	פְּצִירָה (נ)
nail clippers	gozez tsipor'nayim	גּוֹזֵז צִיפּוֹרְנַיִים (ז)
tweezers	pin'tseta	פִּינְצֶטָה (נ)

cosmetics	tamrukim	תַּמְרוּקִים (ז"ר)
face mask	masexa	מַסֵּכָה (נ)
manicure	manikur	מָנִיקוּר (ז)
to have a manicure	laʻasot manikur	לַעֲשׂוֹת מָנִיקוּר
pedicure	pedikur	פֶּדִיקוּר (ז)
make-up bag	tik ipur	תִּיק אִיפּוּר (ז)
face powder	'pudra	פּוּדְרָה (נ)
powder compact	pudriya	פּוּדְרִיָּה (נ)
blusher	'somek	סוֹמֶק (ז)
perfume (bottled)	'bosem	בּוֹשֶׂם (ז)
toilet water (lotion)	mei 'bosem	מֵי בּוֹשֶׂם (ז"ר)
lotion	mei panim	מֵי פָּנִים (ז"ר)
cologne	mei 'bosem	מֵי בּוֹשֶׂם (ז"ר)
eyeshadow	tslalit	צְלָלִית (נ)
eyeliner	ai 'lainer	אַי לַיינֶר (ז)
mascara	'maskara	מַסְקָרָה (נ)
lipstick	sfaton	שְׂפָתוֹן (ז)
nail polish, enamel	'laka letsipor'nayim	לַכָּה לְצִיפּוֹרְנַיִים (נ)
hair spray	tarsis lese'ar	תַּרְסִיס לְשֵׂיעָר (ז)
deodorant	de'odo'rant	דֵּאוֹדוֹרַנְט (ז)
cream	krem	קְרֶם (ז)
face cream	krem panim	קְרֶם פָּנִים (ז)
hand cream	krem ya'dayim	קְרֶם יָדַיִים (ז)
anti-wrinkle cream	krem 'neged kmatim	קְרֶם נֶגֶד קְמָטִים (ז)
day cream	krem yom	קְרֶם יוֹם (ז)
night cream	krem 'laila	קְרֶם לַיְלָה (ז)
day (as adj)	yomi	יוֹמִי
night (as adj)	leili	לֵילִי
tampon	tampon	טַמְפּוֹן (ז)
toilet paper (toilet roll)	neyar tu'alet	נְיָיר טוּאָלֶט (ז)
hair dryer	meyabeʃ se'ar	מְיַבֵּשׁ שֵׂיעָר (ז)

34. Watches. Clocks

watch (wristwatch)	ʃe'on yad	שְׁעוֹן יָד (ז)
dial	'luax ʃa'on	לוּחַ שָׁעוֹן (ז)
hand (of clock, watch)	maxog	מָחוֹג (ז)
metal watch band	tsamid	צָמִיד (ז)
watch strap	retsu'a leʃa'on	רְצוּעָה לְשָׁעוֹן (נ)
battery	solela	סוֹלְלָה (נ)
to be dead (battery)	lehitroken	לְהִתְרוֹקֵן
to change a battery	lehaxlif	לְהַחְלִיף
to run fast	lemaher	לְמַהֵר

to run slow	lefager	לְפַגֵּר
wall clock	ʃeʿon kir	שְׁעוֹן קִיר (ז)
hourglass	ʃeʿon χol	שְׁעוֹן חוֹל (ז)
sundial	ʃeʿon ʃemeʃ	שְׁעוֹן שֶׁמֶשׁ (ז)
alarm clock	ʃaʿon meʿorer	שְׁעוֹן מְעוֹרֵר (ז)
watchmaker	ʃaʿan	שַׁעָן (ז)
to repair (vt)	letaken	לְתַקֵּן

Food. Nutricion

35. Food

meat	basar	בָּשָׂר (ז)
chicken	of	עוֹף (ז)
Rock Cornish hen (poussin)	pargit	פַּרְגִית (נ)
duck	barvaz	בַּרְוָז (ז)
goose	avaz	אֲוָז (ז)
game	'tsayid	צַיִד (ז)
turkey	'hodu	הוֹדוּ (ז)
pork	basar xazir	בְּשַׂר חֲזִיר (ז)
veal	basar 'egel	בְּשַׂר עֵגֶל (ז)
lamb	basar 'keves	בְּשַׂר כֶּבֶשׂ (ז)
beef	bakar	בָּקָר (ז)
rabbit	arnav	אַרְנָב (ז)
sausage (bologna, pepperoni, etc.)	naknik	נַקְנִיק (ז)
vienna sausage (frankfurter)	naknikiya	נַקְנִיקִיָה (נ)
bacon	'kotel xazir	קוֹתֶל חֲזִיר (ז)
ham	basar xazir me'uʃan	בְּשַׂר חֲזִיר מְעוּשָן (ז)
gammon	'kotel xazir me'uʃan	קוֹתֶל חֲזִיר מְעוּשָן (ז)
pâté	pate	פָּטֶה (ז)
liver	kaved	כָּבֵד (ז)
hamburger (ground beef)	basar taxun	בְּשַׂר טָחוּן (ז)
tongue	laʃon	לָשוֹן (נ)
egg	beitsa	בֵּיצָה (נ)
eggs	beitsim	בֵּיצִים (ז"ר)
egg white	xelbon	חֶלְבּוֹן (ז)
egg yolk	xelmon	חֶלְמוֹן (ז)
fish	dag	דָג (ז)
seafood	perot yam	פֵּירוֹת יָם (ז"ר)
crustaceans	sartana'im	סַרְטָנָאִים (ז"ר)
caviar	kavyar	קַוְויָאר (ז)
crab	sartan yam	סַרְטָן יָם (ז)
shrimp	ʃrimps	שְרִימְפְּס (ז"ר)
oyster	tsidpat ma'axal	צִדְפַּת מַאֲכָל (נ)
spiny lobster	'lobster kotsani	לוֹבְּסְטֶר קוֹצָנִי (ז)

octopus	tamnun	תַמְנוּן (ז)
squid	kala'mari	קָלָמָארִי (ז)
sturgeon	basar haxidkan	בְּשַׂר הַחִדְקָן (ז)
salmon	'salmon	סַלְמוֹן (ז)
halibut	putit	פּוּטִית (נ)
cod	ʃibut	שִׁיבּוּט (ז)
mackerel	kolyas	קוֹלְיָס (ז)
tuna	'tuna	טוּנָה (נ)
eel	tslofax	צְלוֹפָח (ז)
trout	forel	פוֹרֶל (ז)
sardine	sardin	סַרְדִין (ז)
pike	ze'ev 'mayim	זְאֵב מַיִם (ז)
herring	ma'liax	מָלִיחַ (ז)
bread	'lexem	לֶחֶם (ז)
cheese	gvina	גְבִינָה (נ)
sugar	sukar	סוּכָּר (ז)
salt	'melax	מֶלַח (ז)
rice	'orez	אוֹרֶז (ז)
pasta (macaroni)	'pasta	פַּסְטָה (נ)
noodles	irtiyot	אִטְרִיוֹת (נ"ר)
butter	xem'a	חֶמְאָה (נ)
vegetable oil	'ʃemen tsimxi	שֶׁמֶן צִמְחִי (ז)
sunflower oil	'ʃemen xamaniyot	שֶׁמֶן חַמָנִיוֹת (ז)
margarine	marga'rina	מַרְגָרִינָה (נ)
olives	zeitim	זֵיתִים (ז"ר)
olive oil	'ʃemen 'zayit	שֶׁמֶן זַיִת (ז)
milk	xalav	חָלָב (ז)
condensed milk	xalav merukaz	חָלָב מְרוּכָּז (ז)
yogurt	'yogurt	יוֹגוּרט (ז)
sour cream	ʃa'menet	שַׁמֶנֶת (נ)
cream (of milk)	ʃa'menet	שַׁמֶנֶת (נ)
mayonnaise	mayonez	מָיוֹנֵז (ז)
buttercream	ka'tsefet xem'a	קַצֶפֶת חֶמְאָה (נ)
cereal grains (wheat, etc.)	grisim	גְרִיסִים (ז"ר)
flour	'kemax	קֶמַח (ז)
canned food	ʃimurim	שִׁימוּרִים (ז"ר)
cornflakes	ptitei 'tiras	פְּתִיתֵי תִירָס (ז"ר)
honey	dvaʃ	דְבַשׁ (ז)
jam	riba	רִיבָּה (נ)
chewing gum	'mastik	מַסְטִיק (ז)

36. Drinks

water	'mayim	מַיִם (ז״ר)
drinking water	mei ʃtiya	מֵי שְׁתִיָּה (ז״ר)
mineral water	'mayim mine'raliyim	מַיִם מִינֶרָלִיִּים (ז״ר)
still (adj)	lo mugaz	לֹא מוּגָז
carbonated (adj)	mugaz	מוּגָז
sparkling (adj)	mugaz	מוּגָז
ice	'kerax	קֶרַח (ז)
with ice	im 'kerax	עִם קֶרַח
non-alcoholic (adj)	natul alkohol	נְטוּל אַלְכּוֹהוֹל
soft drink	maʃke kal	מַשְׁקֶה קַל (ז)
refreshing drink	maʃke mera'anen	מַשְׁקֶה מְרַעֲנֵן (ז)
lemonade	limo'nada	לִימוֹנָדָה (נ)
liquors	maʃka'ot xarifim	מַשְׁקָאוֹת חֲרִיפִים (ז״ר)
wine	'yayin	יַיִן (ז)
white wine	'yayin lavan	יַיִן לָבָן (ז)
red wine	'yayin adom	יַיִן אָדוֹם (ז)
liqueur	liker	לִיקֶר (ז)
champagne	ʃam'panya	שַׁמְפַּנְיָה (נ)
vermouth	'vermut	וֶרְמוּט (ז)
whiskey	'viski	וִיסְקִי (ז)
vodka	'vodka	וֹדְקָה (נ)
gin	dʒin	גִּ'ין (ז)
cognac	'konyak	קוֹנְיָאק (ז)
rum	rom	רוֹם (ז)
coffee	kafe	קָפֶה (ז)
black coffee	kafe ʃaxor	קָפֶה שָׁחוֹר (ז)
coffee with milk	kafe hafux	קָפֶה הָפוּךְ (ז)
cappuccino	kapu'tʃino	קָפוּצִ'ינוֹ (ז)
instant coffee	kafe names	קָפֶה נָמֵס (ז)
milk	xalav	חָלָב (ז)
cocktail	kokteil	קוֹקְטֵיל (ז)
milkshake	'milkʃeik	מִילְקְשֵׁייק (ז)
juice	mits	מִיץ (ז)
tomato juice	mits agvaniyot	מִיץ עַגְבָנִיּוֹת (ז)
orange juice	mits tapuzim	מִיץ תַּפּוּזִים (ז)
freshly squeezed juice	mits saxut	מִיץ סָחוּט (ז)
beer	'bira	בִּירָה (נ)
light beer	'bira bahira	בִּירָה בְּהִירָה (נ)
dark beer	'bira keha	בִּירָה כֵּהָה (נ)
tea	te	תֵּה (ז)

black tea	te ʃaxor	תֶה שָחוֹר (ז)
green tea	te yarok	תֶה יָרוֹק (ז)

37. Vegetables

vegetables	yerakot	יְרָקוֹת (ז״ר)
greens	'yerek	יֶרֶק (ז)
tomato	agvaniya	עַגבָנִיָה (נ)
cucumber	melafefon	מְלָפְפוֹן (ז)
carrot	'gezer	גֶזֶר (ז)
potato	ta'puax adama	תַפוּחַ אֲדָמָה (ז)
onion	batsal	בָּצָל (ז)
garlic	ʃum	שׁוּם (ז)
cabbage	kruv	כּרוּב (ז)
cauliflower	kruvit	כּרוּבִית (נ)
Brussels sprouts	kruv nitsanim	כּרוּב נִצָנִים (ז)
broccoli	'brokoli	בּרוֹקוֹלִי (ז)
beetroot	'selek	סֶלֶק (ז)
eggplant	xatsil	חָצִיל (ז)
zucchini	kiʃu	קִישוּא (ז)
pumpkin	'dla'at	דלַעַת (נ)
turnip	'lefet	לֶפֶת (נ)
parsley	petro'zilya	פֶּטרוֹזִילִיָה (נ)
dill	ʃamir	שָמִיר (ז)
lettuce	'xasa	חַסָה (נ)
celery	'seleri	סֶלֶרִי (ז)
asparagus	aspa'ragos	אַספָּרָגוֹס (ז)
spinach	'tered	תֶרֶד (ז)
pea	afuna	אֲפוּנָה (נ)
beans	pol	פוֹל (ז)
corn (maize)	'tiras	תִירָס (ז)
kidney bean	ʃu'it	שְעוּעִית (נ)
bell pepper	'pilpel	פִּלפֵּל (ז)
radish	tsnonit	צנוֹנִית (נ)
artichoke	artiʃok	אַרטִישוֹק (ז)

38. Fruits. Nuts

fruit	pri	פּרִי (ז)
apple	ta'puax	תַפּוּחַ (ז)
pear	agas	אַגָס (ז)
lemon	limon	לִימוֹן (ז)

| orange | tapuz | תַפּוּז (ז) |
| strawberry (garden ~) | tut sade | תּוּת שָׂדֶה (ז) |

mandarin	klemen'tina	קְלֶמֶנְטִינָה (נ)
plum	ʃezif	שְׁזִיף (ז)
peach	afarsek	אֲפַרְסֵק (ז)
apricot	'miʃmeʃ	מִשְׁמֵשׁ (ז)
raspberry	'petel	פֶּטֶל (ז)
pineapple	'ananas	אֲנָנָס (ז)

banana	ba'nana	בָּנָנָה (נ)
watermelon	ava'tiaχ	אֲבַטִּיחַ (ז)
grape	anavim	עֲנָבִים (ז״ר)
sour cherry	duvdevan	דוּבְדְּבָן (ז)
sweet cherry	gudgedan	גּוּדְגְּדָן (ז)
melon	melon	מֶלוֹן (ז)

grapefruit	eʃkolit	אֶשְׁכּוֹלִית (נ)
avocado	avo'kado	אֲבוֹקָדוֹ (ז)
papaya	pa'paya	פַּפָּאיָה (נ)
mango	'mango	מַנְגוֹ (ז)
pomegranate	rimon	רִימוֹן (ז)

redcurrant	dumdemanit aduma	דּוּמְדְּמָנִית אֲדוּמָה (נ)
blackcurrant	dumdemanit ʃχora	דּוּמְדְּמָנִית שְׁחוֹרָה (נ)
gooseberry	χazarzar	חֲזַרְזַר (ז)
bilberry	uχmanit	אוּכְמָנִית (נ)
blackberry	'petel ʃaχor	פֶּטֶל שָׁחוֹר (ז)

raisin	tsimukim	צִימוּקִים (ז״ר)
fig	te'ena	תְּאֵנָה (נ)
date	tamar	תָּמָר (ז)

peanut	botnim	בּוֹטְנִים (ז״ר)
almond	ʃaked	שָׁקֵד (ז)
walnut	egoz 'meleχ	אֱגוֹז מֶלֶךְ (ז)
hazelnut	egoz ilsar	אֱגוֹז אִלְסָר (ז)
coconut	'kokus	קוֹקוּס (ז)
pistachios	'fistuk	פִּיסְטוּק (ז)

39. Bread. Candy

bakers' confectionery (pastry)	mutsrei kondi'torya	מוּצְרֵי קוֹנְדִיטוֹרְיָה (ז״ר)
bread	'leχem	לֶחֶם (ז)
cookies	ugiya	עוּגִיָּה (נ)

chocolate (n)	'ʃokolad	שׁוֹקוֹלָד (ז)
chocolate (as adj)	mi'ʃokolad	מִשׁוֹקוֹלָד
candy (wrapped)	sukariya	סוּכָּרִיָּה (נ)

cake (e.g., cupcake)	uga	עוּגָה (נ)
cake (e.g., birthday ~)	uga	עוּגָה (נ)
pie (e.g., apple ~)	pai	פַּאי (ז)
filling (for cake, pie)	milui	מִילוּי (ז)
jam (whole fruit jam)	riba	רִיבָּה (נ)
marmalade	marme'lada	מַרְמֶלָדָה (נ)
waffles	'vaflim	וַפְלִים (ז"ר)
ice-cream	'glida	גְלִידָה (נ)
pudding	'puding	פּוּדִינג (ז)

40. Cooked dishes

course, dish	mana	מָנָה (נ)
cuisine	mitbax	מִטְבָּח (ז)
recipe	matkon	מַתכּוֹן (ז)
portion	mana	מָנָה (נ)
salad	salat	סָלָט (ז)
soup	marak	מָרָק (ז)
clear soup (broth)	marak tsax, tsir	מָרָק צַח, צִיר (ז)
sandwich (bread)	karix	כָּרִיך (ז)
fried eggs	beitsat ain	בֵּיצַת עַיִן (נ)
hamburger (beefburger)	'hamburger	הַמְבּוּרְגֶר (ז)
beefsteak	umtsa, steik	אוּמְצָה (נ), סטֵייק (ז)
side dish	to'sefet	תוֹסֶפֶת (נ)
spaghetti	spa'geti	סְפָּגֶטִי (ז)
mashed potatoes	mexit tapuxei adama	מְחִית תַפּוּחֵי אֲדָמָה (נ)
pizza	'pitsa	פִּיצָה (נ)
porridge (oatmeal, etc.)	daysa	דַייסָה (נ)
omelet	xavita	חֲבִיתָה (נ)
boiled (e.g., ~ beef)	mevuʃal	מְבוּשָל
smoked (adj)	me'uʃan	מְעוּשָן
fried (adj)	metugan	מְטוּגָן
dried (adj)	meyubaʃ	מְיוּבָּש
frozen (adj)	kafu	קָפוּא
pickled (adj)	kavuʃ	כָּבוּש
sweet (sugary)	matok	מָתוֹק
salty (adj)	ma'luax	מָלוּחַ
cold (adj)	kar	קַר
hot (adj)	xam	חַם
bitter (adj)	marir	מָרִיר
tasty (adj)	ta'im	טָעִים
to cook in boiling water	levaʃel be'mayim rotxim	לְבַשֵל בְּמַיִם רוֹתחִים

to cook (dinner)	levaʃel	לְבַשֵׁל
to fry (vt)	letagen	לְטַגֵן
to heat up (food)	leχamem	לְחַמֵם
to salt (vt)	leham'liaχ	לְהַמְלִיחַ
to pepper (vt)	lefalpel	לְפַלְפֵּל
to grate (vt)	lerasek	לְרַסֵק
peel (n)	klipa	קְלִיפָה (נ)
to peel (vt)	lekalef	לְקַלֵף

41. Spices

salt	'melaχ	מֶלַח (ז)
salty (adj)	ma'luaχ	מָלוּחַ
to salt (vt)	leham'liaχ	לְהַמְלִיחַ
black pepper	'pilpel ʃaχor	פִּלְפֵּל שָׁחוֹר (ז)
red pepper (milled ~)	'pilpel adom	פִּלְפֵּל אָדוֹם (ז)
mustard	χardal	חַרְדָל (ז)
horseradish	χa'zeret	חֲזֶרֶת (נ)
condiment	'rotev	רוֹטֶב (ז)
spice	tavlin	תַבְלִין (ז)
sauce	'rotev	רוֹטֶב (ז)
vinegar	'χomets	חוֹמֶץ (ז)
anise	kamnon	כַּמְנוֹן (ז)
basil	reχan	רֵיחָן (ז)
cloves	tsi'poren	צִיפּוֹרֶן (ז)
ginger	'dʒindʒer	גִ'ינגֶ'ר (ז)
coriander	'kusbara	כּוּסְבָּרָה (נ)
cinnamon	kinamon	קִינָמוֹן (ז)
sesame	'ʃumʃum	שׁוּמשׁוֹם (ז)
bay leaf	ale dafna	עָלֶה דַפְנָה (ז)
paprika	'paprika	פַּפְּרִיקָה (נ)
caraway	'kimel	קִימָל (ז)
saffron	ze'afran	זְעַפְרָן (ז)

42. Meals

food	'oχel	אוֹכֶל (ז)
to eat (vi, vt)	le'eχol	לֶאֱכוֹל
breakfast	aruχat 'boker	אֲרוּחַת בּוֹקֶר (נ)
to have breakfast	le'eχol aruχat 'boker	לֶאֱכוֹל אֲרוּחַת בּוֹקֶר
lunch	aruχat tsaha'rayim	אֲרוּחַת צָהֳרַיִים (נ)
to have lunch	le'eχol aruχat tsaha'rayim	לֶאֱכוֹל אֲרוּחַת צָהֳרַיִים

dinner	aruxat 'erev	אֲרוּחַת עֶרֶב (נ)
to have dinner	le'exol aruxat 'erev	לֶאֱכוֹל אֲרוּחַת עֶרֶב
appetite	te'avon	תֵּיאָבוֹן (ז)
Enjoy your meal!	betei'avon!	בְּתֵיאָבוֹן!
to open (~ a bottle)	liftoax	לִפתוֹחַ
to spill (liquid)	lifpox	לִשפּוֹך
to spill out (vi)	lehifapex	לְהִישָׁפֵּך
to boil (vi)	lir'toax	לִרתוֹחַ
to boil (vt)	lehar'tiax	לְהַרתִיחַ
boiled (~ water)	ra'tuax	רָתוּחַ
to chill, cool down (vt)	lekarer	לְקָרֵר
to chill (vi)	lehitkarer	לְהִתקָרֵר
taste, flavor	'ta'am	טַעַם (ז)
aftertaste	'ta'am levai	טַעַם לְוואי (ז)
to slim down (lose weight)	lirzot	לִרזוֹת
diet	di''eta	דִיאֶטָה (נ)
vitamin	vitamin	וִיטָמִין (ז)
calorie	ka'lorya	קָלוֹרִיָה (נ)
vegetarian (n)	tsimxoni	צִמחוֹנִי (ז)
vegetarian (adj)	tsimxoni	צִמחוֹנִי
fats (nutrient)	fumanim	שוּמָנִים (ז"ר)
proteins	xelbonim	חֶלבּוֹנִים (ז"ר)
carbohydrates	paxmema	פַּחמִימָה (נ)
slice (of lemon, ham)	prusa	פרוּסָה (נ)
piece (of cake, pie)	xatixa	חֲתִיכָה (נ)
crumb (of bread, cake, etc.)	perur	פֵּירוּר (ז)

43. Table setting

spoon	kaf	כַּף (נ)
knife	sakin	סַכִּין (ז, נ)
fork	mazleg	מַזלֵג (ז)
cup (e.g., coffee ~)	'sefel	סֵפֶל (ז)
plate (dinner ~)	tsa'laxat	צַלַחַת (נ)
saucer	taxtit	תַחתִית (נ)
napkin (on table)	mapit	מַפִּית (נ)
toothpick	keisam fi'nayim	קֵיסָם שִינַיִים (ז)

44. Restaurant

restaurant	mis'ada	מִסעָדָה (נ)
coffee house	beit kafe	בֵּית קָפֶה (ז)

pub, bar	bar, pab	בָּר, פָּאב (ז)
tearoom	beit te	בֵּית תֶה (ז)
waiter	meltsar	מֶלְצָר (ז)
waitress	meltsarit	מֶלְצָרִית (נ)
bartender	'barmen	בַּרמֶן (ז)
menu	tafrit	תַפרִיט (ז)
wine list	reʃimat yeynot	רְשִׁימַת יֵינוֹת (נ)
to book a table	lehazmin ʃulχan	לְהַזמִין שׁוּלחָן
course, dish	mana	מָנָה (נ)
to order (meal)	lehazmin	לְהַזמִין
to make an order	lehazmin	לְהַזמִין
aperitif	maʃke meta'aven	מַשׁקֶה מְתָאָבֵן (ז)
appetizer	meta'aven	מְתָאָבֵן (ז)
dessert	ki'nuaχ	קִינוּחַ (ז)
check	χeʃbon	חֶשׁבּוֹן (ז)
to pay the check	leʃalem	לְשַׁלֵם
to give change	latet 'odef	לָתֵת עוֹדֶף
tip	tip	טִיפּ (ז)

Family, relatives and friends

45. Personal information. Forms

name (first name)	ʃem	שֵׁם (ז)
surname (last name)	ʃem miʃpaχa	שֵׁם מִשְׁפָּחָה (ז)
date of birth	ta'ariχ leda	תַאֲרִיךְ לֵידָה (ז)
place of birth	mekom leda	מְקוֹם לֵידָה (ז)
nationality	le'om	לְאוֹם (ז)
place of residence	mekom megurim	מְקוֹם מְגוּרִים (ז)
country	medina	מְדִינָה (נ)
profession (occupation)	mik'tso'a	מִקְצוֹעַ (ז)
gender, sex	min	מִין (ז)
height	'gova	גוֹבַהּ (ז)
weight	miʃkal	מִשְׁקָל (ז)

46. Family members. Relatives

mother	em	אֵם (נ)
father	av	אָב (ז)
son	ben	בֵּן (ז)
daughter	bat	בַּת (נ)
younger daughter	habat haktana	הַבַּת הַקְטָנָה (נ)
younger son	haben hakatan	הַבֵּן הַקָטָן (ז)
eldest daughter	habat habχora	הַבַּת הַבְּכוֹרָה (נ)
eldest son	haben habχor	הַבֵּן הַבְּכוֹר (ז)
brother	aχ	אָח (ז)
elder brother	aχ gadol	אָח גָדוֹל (ז)
younger brother	aχ katan	אָח קָטָן (ז)
sister	aχot	אָחוֹת (נ)
elder sister	aχot gdola	אָחוֹת גדוֹלָה (נ)
younger sister	aχot ktana	אָחוֹת קְטָנָה (נ)
cousin (masc.)	ben dod	בֶּן דוֹד (ז)
cousin (fem.)	bat 'doda	בַּת דוֹדָה (נ)
mom, mommy	'ima	אִמָא (נ)
dad, daddy	'aba	אַבָּא (ז)
parents	horim	הוֹרִים (ז״ר)
child	'yeled	יֶלֶד (ז)
children	yeladim	יְלָדִים (ז״ר)

grandmother	'savta	סָבְתָא (נ)
grandfather	'saba	סַבָּא (ז)
grandson	'neχed	נֶכֶד (ז)
granddaughter	neχda	נֶכְדָה (נ)
grandchildren	neχadim	נְכָדִים (ז"ר)
uncle	dod	דוֹד (ז)
aunt	'doda	דוֹדָה (נ)
nephew	aχyan	אַחְיָן (ז)
niece	aχyanit	אַחְיָנִית (נ)
mother-in-law (wife's mother)	χamot	חָמוֹת (נ)
father-in-law (husband's father)	χam	חָם (ז)
son-in-law (daughter's husband)	χatan	חָתָן (ז)
stepmother	em χoreget	אֵם חוֹרֶגֶת (נ)
stepfather	av χoreg	אָב חוֹרֵג (ז)
infant	tinok	תִּינוֹק (ז)
baby (infant)	tinok	תִּינוֹק (ז)
little boy, kid	pa'ot	פָּעוֹט (ז)
wife	iʃa	אִשָׁה (נ)
husband	'ba'al	בַּעַל (ז)
spouse (husband)	ben zug	בֶּן זוּג (ז)
spouse (wife)	bat zug	בַּת זוּג (נ)
married (masc.)	nasui	נָשׂוּי
married (fem.)	nesu'a	נְשׂוּאָה
single (unmarried)	ravak	רַוָוק
bachelor	ravak	רַוָוק (ז)
divorced (masc.)	garuʃ	גָרוּשׁ
widow	almana	אַלְמָנָה (נ)
widower	alman	אַלְמָן (ז)
relative	karov miʃpaχa	קָרוֹב מִשְׁפָּחָה (ז)
close relative	karov miʃpaχa	קָרוֹב מִשְׁפָּחָה (ז)
distant relative	karov raχok	קָרוֹב רָחוֹק (ז)
relatives	krovei miʃpaχa	קְרוֹבֵי מִשְׁפָּחָה (ז"ר)
orphan (boy)	yatom	יָתוֹם (ז)
orphan (girl)	yetoma	יְתוֹמָה (נ)
guardian (of a minor)	apo'tropos	אֲפּוֹטְרוֹפּוֹס (ז)
to adopt (a boy)	le'amets	לְאַמֵץ
to adopt (a girl)	le'amets	לְאַמֵץ

Medicine

47. Diseases

sickness	maxala	מַחֲלָה (נ)
to be sick	lihyot xole	לִהיוֹת חוֹלֶה
health	bri'ut	בּרִיאוּת (נ)
runny nose (coryza)	na'zelet	נַזֶלֶת (נ)
tonsillitis	da'leket ʃkedim	דַלֶקֶת שקֵדִים (נ)
cold (illness)	hitstanenut	הִצטַנְנוּת (נ)
to catch a cold	lehitstanen	לְהִצטַנֵן
bronchitis	bron'xitis	בּרוֹנכִיטִיס (ז)
pneumonia	da'leket re'ot	דַלֶקֶת רֵיאוֹת (נ)
flu, influenza	ʃa'pa'at	שַפַּעַת (נ)
nearsighted (adj)	ktsar re'iya	קצַר רְאִייָה
farsighted (adj)	rexok re'iya	רְחוֹק־רְאִייָה
strabismus (crossed eyes)	pzila	פּזִילָה (נ)
cross-eyed (adj)	pozel	פּוֹזֵל
cataract	katarakt	קָטָרַקט (ז)
glaucoma	gla'u'koma	גלָאוּקוֹמָה (נ)
stroke	ʃavats moxi	שָבָץ מוֹחִי (ז)
heart attack	hetkef lev	הֶתקֵף לֵב (ז)
myocardial infarction	'otem ʃrir halev	אוֹטֶם שרִיר הַלֵב (ז)
paralysis	ʃituk	שִיתוּק (ז)
to paralyze (vt)	leʃatek	לְשַתֵק
allergy	a'lergya	אָלֶרגיָה (נ)
asthma	'astma, ka'tseret	אַסתמָה, קַצֶרֶת (נ)
diabetes	su'keret	סוּכֶּרֶת (נ)
toothache	ke'ev ʃi'nayim	כּאֵב שִינַיים (ז)
caries	a'ʃeʃet	עַשֶשֶת (נ)
diarrhea	ʃilʃul	שִלשוּל (ז)
constipation	atsirut	עֲצִירוּת (נ)
stomach upset	kilkul keiva	קִלקוּל קֵיבָה (ז)
food poisoning	har'alat mazon	הַרעָלַת מָזוֹן (נ)
to get food poisoning	laxatof har'alat mazon	לַחֲטוֹף הַרעָלַת מָזוֹן
arthritis	da'leket mifrakim	דַלֶקֶת מִפרָקִים (נ)
rickets	ra'kexet	רַכֶּכֶת (נ)
rheumatism	ʃigaron	שִיגָרוֹן (ז)

atherosclerosis	ar'teryo skle'rosis	אַרְטֶרְיוֹ־סְקְלֶרוֹסִיס (ז)
gastritis	da'leket keiva	דַלֶקֶת קֵיבָה (נ)
appendicitis	da'leket toseftan	דַלֶקֶת תוֹסֶפְתָן (נ)
cholecystitis	da'leket kis hamara	דַלֶקֶת כִּיס הַמָרָה (נ)
ulcer	'ulkus, kiv	אוֹלקוּס, כִּיב (ז)
measles	χa'tsevet	חַצֶבֶת (נ)
rubella (German measles)	a'demet	אַדֶמֶת (נ)
jaundice	tsa'hevet	צָהֶבֶת (נ)
hepatitis	da'leket kaved	דַלֶקֶת כָּבֵד (נ)
schizophrenia	sχizo'frenya	סְכִיזוֹפְרֶנְיָה (נ)
rabies (hydrophobia)	ka'levet	כַּלֶבֶת (נ)
neurosis	noi'roza	נוֹירוֹזָה (נ)
concussion	za'a'zu'a 'moaχ	זַעֲזוּעַ מוֹחַ (ז)
cancer	sartan	סַרְטָן (ז)
sclerosis	ta'refet	טָרֶשֶת (נ)
multiple sclerosis	ta'refet nefotsa	טָרֶשֶת נְפוֹצָה (נ)
alcoholism	alkoholizm	אַלכּוֹהוֹלִיזם (ז)
alcoholic (n)	alkoholist	אַלכּוֹהוֹלִיסט (ז)
syphilis	a'gevet	עַגֶבֶת (נ)
AIDS	eids	אַיידס (ז)
tumor	gidul	גִידוּל (ז)
malignant (adj)	mam'ir	מַמאִיר
benign (adj)	ʃapir	שַפִיר
fever	ka'daχat	קַדַחַת (נ)
malaria	ma'larya	מָלַרְיָה (נ)
gangrene	gan'grena	גַנגרֶנָה (נ)
seasickness	maχalat yam	מַחֲלַת יָם (נ)
epilepsy	maχalat hanefila	מַחֲלַת הַנְפִילָה (נ)
epidemic	magefa	מַגֵיפָה (נ)
typhus	'tifus	טִיפוּס (ז)
tuberculosis	ʃa'χefet	שַחֶפֶת (נ)
cholera	ko'lera	כּוֹלֵרָה (נ)
plague (bubonic ~)	davar	דֶבֶר (ז)

48. Symptoms. Treatments. Part 1

symptom	simptom	סִימפטוֹם (ז)
temperature	χom	חוֹם (ז)
high temperature (fever)	χom ga'voha	חוֹם גָבוֹהַ (ז)
pulse	'dofek	דוֹפֶק (ז)
dizziness (vertigo)	sχar'χoret	סחַרחוֹרֶת (נ)
hot (adj)	χam	חַם

shivering	tsmar'moret	צְמַרמוֹרֶת (ז)
pale (e.g., ~ face)	xiver	חִיווֵר
cough	ʃi'ul	שִיעוּל (ז)
to cough (vi)	lehiʃta'el	לְהִשתָעֵל
to sneeze (vi)	lehit'ateʃ	לְהִתעַטֵש
faint	ilafon	עִילָפוֹן (ז)
to faint (vi)	lehit'alef	לְהִתעַלֵף
bruise (hématome)	xabura	חַבּוּרָה (נ)
bump (lump)	blita	בּלִיטָה (נ)
to bang (bump)	lekabel maka	לְקַבֵּל מַכָּה
contusion (bruise)	maka	מַכָּה (נ)
to get a bruise	lekabel maka	לְקַבֵּל מַכָּה
to limp (vi)	lits'lo'a	לְצלוֹעַ
dislocation	'neka	נֶקַע (ז)
to dislocate (vt)	lin'ko'a	לִנקוֹעַ
fracture	'ʃever	שֶבֶר (ז)
to have a fracture	liʃbor	לִשבּוֹר
cut (e.g., paper ~)	xatax	חָתָך (ז)
to cut oneself	lehixatex	לְהֵיחָתֵך
bleeding	dimum	דִימוּם (ז)
burn (injury)	kviya	כּווִייָה (נ)
to get burned	laxatof kviya	לַחֲטוֹף כּווִייָה
to prick (vt)	lidkor	לִדקוֹר
to prick oneself	lehidaker	לְהִידָקֵר
to injure (vt)	lif'tso'a	לִפצוֹעַ
injury	ptsi'a	פּצִיעָה (נ)
wound	'petsa	פֶּצַע (ז)
trauma	'tra'uma	טרָאוּמָה (נ)
to be delirious	lahazot	לַהֲזוֹת
to stutter (vi)	legamgem	לְגַמגֵם
sunstroke	makat 'ʃemeʃ	מַכַּת שֶמֶש (נ)

49. Symptoms. Treatments. Part 2

pain, ache	ke'ev	כְּאֵב (ז)
splinter (in foot, etc.)	kots	קוֹץ (ז)
sweat (perspiration)	ze'a	זִיעָה (נ)
to sweat (perspire)	leha'zi'a	לְהַזִיעַ
vomiting	haka'a	הֲקָאָה (נ)
convulsions	pirkusim	פִּירכּוּסִים (ז״ר)
pregnant (adj)	hara	הָרָה
to be born	lehivaled	לְהִיווָלֵד

delivery, labor	leda	לֵידָה (נ)
to deliver (~ a baby)	la'ledet	לָלֶדֶת
abortion	hapala	הַפָּלָה (נ)
breathing, respiration	neʃima	נְשִׁימָה (נ)
in-breath (inhalation)	ʃe'ifa	שְׁאִיפָה (נ)
out-breath (exhalation)	neʃifa	נְשִׁיפָה (נ)
to exhale (breathe out)	linʃof	לִנשׁוֹף
to inhale (vi)	liʃ'of	לִשׁאוֹף
disabled person	naxe	נָכֶה (ז)
cripple	naxe	נָכֶה (ז)
drug addict	narkoman	נַרקוֹמָן (ז)
deaf (adj)	xereʃ	חֵירֵשׁ
mute (adj)	ilem	אִילֵם
deaf mute (adj)	xereʃ-ilem	חֵירֵשׁ-אִילֵם
mad, insane (adj)	meʃuga	מְשׁוּגָע
madman (demented person)	meʃuga	מְשׁוּגָע (ז)
madwoman	meʃu'ga'at	מְשׁוּגַעַת (נ)
to go insane	lehiʃta'ge'a	לְהִשׁתַגֵעַ
gene	gen	גֵן (ז)
immunity	xasinut	חָסִינוּת (נ)
hereditary (adj)	toraʃti	תוֹרַשׁתִי
congenital (adj)	mulad	מוּלָד
virus	'virus	וִירוּס (ז)
microbe	xaidak	חַיידָק (ז)
bacterium	bak'terya	בַּקטֶריָה (נ)
infection	zihum	זִיהוּם (ז)

50. Symptoms. Treatments. Part 3

hospital	beit xolim	בֵּית חוֹלִים (ז)
patient	metupal	מְטוּפָּל (ז)
diagnosis	avxana	אַבחָנָה (נ)
cure	ripui	רִיפּוּי (ז)
medical treatment	tipul refu'i	טִיפּוּל רְפוּאִי (ז)
to get treatment	lekabel tipul	לְקַבֵּל טִיפּוּל
to treat (~ a patient)	letapel be...	לְטַפֵּל בְּ...
to nurse (look after)	letapel be...	לְטַפֵּל בְּ...
care (nursing ~)	tipul	טִיפּוּל (ז)
operation, surgery	ni'tuax	נִיתוּחַ (ז)
to bandage (head, limb)	laxboʃ	לַחבּוֹשׁ
bandaging	xaviʃa	חֲבִישָׁה (נ)

vaccination	xisun	חִיסוּן (ז)
to vaccinate (vt)	lexasen	לְחַסֵן
injection, shot	zrika	זְרִיקָה (נ)
to give an injection	lehazrik	לְהַזְרִיק
attack	hetkef	הֶתְקֵף (ז)
amputation	kti'a	קְטִיעָה (נ)
to amputate (vt)	lik'to'a	לִקְטוֹעַ
coma	tar'demet	תַרְדֶמֶת (נ)
to be in a coma	lihyot betar'demet	לִהיוֹת בְּתַרְדֶמֶת
intensive care	tipul nimrats	טִיפּוּל נִמרָץ (ז)
to recover (~ from flu)	lehaxlim	לְהַחלִים
condition (patient's ~)	matsav	מַצָב (ז)
consciousness	hakara	הַכָּרָה (נ)
memory (faculty)	zikaron	זִיכָּרוֹן (ז)
to pull out (tooth)	la'akor	לַעֲקוֹר
filling	stima	סתִימָה (נ)
to fill (a tooth)	la'asot stima	לַעֲשׂוֹת סתִימָה
hypnosis	hip'noza	הִיפּנוֹזָה (נ)
to hypnotize (vt)	lehapnet	לְהַפנֵט

51. Doctors

doctor	rofe	רוֹפֵא (ז)
nurse	axot	אָחוֹת (נ)
personal doctor	rofe iʃi	רוֹפֵא אִישִי (ז)
dentist	rofe ʃi'nayim	רוֹפֵא שִינַיִים (ז)
eye doctor	rofe ei'nayim	רוֹפֵא עֵינַיִים (ז)
internist	rofe pnimi	רוֹפֵא פְּנִימִי (ז)
surgeon	kirurg	כִּירוּרג (ז)
psychiatrist	psixi''ater	פּסִיכִיאָטֶר (ז)
pediatrician	rofe yeladim	רוֹפֵא יְלָדִים (ז)
psychologist	psixolog	פּסִיכוֹלוֹג (ז)
gynecologist	rofe naʃim	רוֹפֵא נָשִים (ז)
cardiologist	kardyolog	קַרדיוֹלוֹג (ז)

52. Medicine. Drugs. Accessories

medicine, drug	trufa	תרוּפָה (נ)
remedy	trufa	תרוּפָה (נ)
to prescribe (vt)	lirʃom	לִרשוֹם
prescription	mirʃam	מִרשָם (ז)
tablet, pill	kadur	כַּדוּר (ז)

ointment	miʃxa	מִשְׁחָה (נ)
ampule	'ampula	אַמְפּוּלָה (נ)
mixture	taʻa'rovet	תַּעֲרוֹבָת (נ)
syrup	sirop	סִירוֹפּ (ז)
pill	gluya	גְלוּיָה (נ)
powder	avka	אַבְקָה (נ)
gauze bandage	tax'boʃet 'gaza	תַחְבּוֹשֶׁת גָאזָה (נ)
cotton wool	'tsemer 'gefen	צֶמֶר גֶפֶן (ז)
iodine	yod	יוֹד (ז)
Band-Aid	'plaster	פְּלַסְטֶר (ז)
eyedropper	taf'tefet	טַפְטֶפֶת (נ)
thermometer	madxom	מַדחוֹם (ז)
syringe	mazrek	מַזְרֵק (ז)
wheelchair	kise galgalim	כִּיסֵא גַלְגַלִים (ז)
crutches	ka'bayim	קַבַּיִים (ז״ר)
painkiller	meʃakex ke'evim	מְשַׁכֵּךְ כְּאֵבִים (ז)
laxative	trufa meʃal'ʃelet	תרוּפָה מְשַׁלְשֶׁלֶת (נ)
spirits (ethanol)	'kohal	כּוֹהַל (ז)
medicinal herbs	isvei marpe	עִשְׂבֵי מַרפֵּא (ז״ר)
herbal (~ tea)	ʃel asavim	שֶׁל עֲשָׂבִים

HUMAN HABITAT

City

53. City. Life in the city

city, town	ir	עִיר (ז)
capital city	ir bira	עִיר בִּירָה (נ)
village	kfar	כְּפָר (ז)
city map	mapat ha'ir	מַפַּת הָעִיר (נ)
downtown	merkaz ha'ir	מֶרכַּז הָעִיר (ז)
suburb	parvar	פַּרוָור (ז)
suburban (adj)	parvari	פַּרוָורִי
outskirts	parvar	פַּרוָור (ז)
environs (suburbs)	svivot	סבִיבוֹת (נ״ר)
city block	ʃxuna	שכוּנָה (נ)
residential block (area)	ʃxunat megurim	שכוּנַת מְגוּרִים (נ)
traffic	tnu'a	תנוּעָה (נ)
traffic lights	ramzor	רַמזוֹר (ז)
public transportation	taxbura tsiburit	תַחבּוּרָה צִיבּוּרִית (נ)
intersection	'tsomet	צוֹמֶת (ז)
crosswalk	ma'avar xatsaya	מַעֲבָר חָצָיָה (ז)
pedestrian underpass	ma'avar tat karka'i	מַעֲבָר תַת־קַרקָעִי (ז)
to cross (~ the street)	laxatsot	לַחֲצוֹת
pedestrian	holex 'regel	הוֹלֵך רֶגֶל (ז)
sidewalk	midraxa	מִדרָכָה (נ)
bridge	'geʃer	גֶשֶר (ז)
embankment (river walk)	ta'yelet	טַיֶילֶת (נ)
fountain	mizraka	מִזרָקָה (נ)
allée (garden walkway)	sdera	שׂדֵרָה (נ)
park	park	פַּארק (ז)
boulevard	sdera	שׂדֵרָה (נ)
square	kikar	כִּיכָּר (נ)
avenue (wide street)	rexov raʃi	רְחוֹב רָאשִי (ז)
street	rexov	רְחוֹב (ז)
side street	simta	סִמטָה (נ)
dead end	mavoi satum	מָבוֹי סָתוּם (ז)
house	'bayit	בַּיִת (ז)
building	binyan	בִּניָין (ז)

skyscraper	gored ʃxakim	גּוֹרֵד שְׁחָקִים (ז)
facade	xazit	חָזִית (נ)
roof	gag	גַּג (ז)
window	xalon	חַלּוֹן (ז)
arch	'keʃet	קֶשֶׁת (נ)
column	amud	עַמּוּד (ז)
corner	pina	פִּינָה (נ)
store window	xalon ra'ava	חַלּוֹן רַאֲוָה (ז)
signboard (store sign, etc.)	'ʃelet	שֶׁלֶט (ז)
poster	kraza	כְּרָזָה (נ)
advertising poster	'poster	פּוֹסְטֶר (ז)
billboard	'luax pirsum	לוּחַ פִּרְסוּם (ז)
garbage, trash	'zevel	זֶבֶל (ז)
trashcan (public ~)	pax aʃpa	פַּח אַשְׁפָּה (ז)
to litter (vi)	lelaxlex	לְלַכְלֵךְ
garbage dump	mizbala	מִזְבָּלָה (נ)
phone booth	ta 'telefon	תָּא טֶלֶפוֹן (ז)
lamppost	amud panas	עַמּוּד פָּנָס (ז)
bench (park ~)	safsal	סַפְסָל (ז)
police officer	ʃoter	שׁוֹטֵר (ז)
police	miʃtara	מִשְׁטָרָה (נ)
beggar	kabtsan	קַבְּצָן (ז)
homeless (n)	xasar 'bayit	חֲסַר בַּיִת (ז)

54. Urban institutions

store	xanut	חֲנוּת (נ)
drugstore, pharmacy	beit mir'kaxat	בֵּית מִרְקַחַת (ז)
eyeglass store	xanut miʃka'fayim	חֲנוּת מִשְׁקָפַיִים (נ)
shopping mall	kanyon	קַנְיוֹן (ז)
supermarket	super'market	סוּפֶּרְמַרְקֶט (ז)
bakery	ma'afiya	מַאֲפִיָּה (נ)
baker	ofe	אוֹפֶה (ז)
pastry shop	xanut mamtakim	חֲנוּת מַמְתַּקִים (נ)
grocery store	ma'kolet	מַכּוֹלֶת (נ)
butcher shop	itliz	אִטְלִיז (ז)
produce store	xanut perot viyerakot	חֲנוּת פֵּירוֹת וִירָקוֹת (נ)
market	ʃuk	שׁוּק (ז)
coffee house	beit kafe	בֵּית קָפֶה (ז)
restaurant	mis'ada	מִסְעָדָה (נ)
pub, bar	pab	פָּאבּ (ז)
pizzeria	pi'tseriya	פִּיצֶּרִיָּה (נ)
hair salon	mispara	מִסְפָּרָה (נ)

post office	'do'ar	דוֹאַר (ז)
dry cleaners	nikui yaveʃ	נִיקוּי יָבֵשׁ (ז)
photo studio	'studyo letsilum	סטוּדיוֹ לְצִילוּם (ז)
shoe store	xanut na'alayim	חֲנוּת נַעֲלַיִים (נ)
bookstore	xanut sfarim	חֲנוּת סְפָרִים (נ)
sporting goods store	xanut sport	חֲנוּת סְפּוֹרט (נ)
clothes repair shop	xanut tikun bgadim	חֲנוּת תִיקוּן בְּגָדִים (נ)
formal wear rental	xanut haskarat bgadim	חֲנוּת הַשׂכָּרַת בְּגָדִים (נ)
video rental store	xanut haʃalat sratim	חֲנוּת הַשׁאָלַת סְרָטִים (נ)
circus	kirkas	קִרקָס (ז)
zoo	gan hayot	גַן חַיוֹת (ז)
movie theater	kol'no'a	קוֹלנוֹעַ (ז)
museum	muze'on	מוּזִיאוֹן (ז)
library	sifriya	סִפרִייָה (נ)
theater	te'atron	תֵיאַטרוֹן (ז)
opera (opera house)	beit 'opera	בֵּית אוֹפֶּרָה (ז)
nightclub	mo'adon 'laila	מוֹעֲדוֹן לַילָה (ז)
casino	ka'zino	קָזִינוֹ (ז)
mosque	misgad	מִסגָד (ז)
synagogue	beit 'kneset	בֵּית הַכּנֶסֶת (ז)
cathedral	kated'rala	קָתֶדרָלָה (נ)
temple	mikdaʃ	מִקדָשׁ (ז)
church	knesiya	כּנֵסִייָה (נ)
college	mixlala	מִכלָלָה (נ)
university	uni'versita	אוּנִיבֶּרסִיטָה (נ)
school	beit 'sefer	בֵּית סֵפֶר (ז)
prefecture	maxoz	מָחוֹז (ז)
city hall	iriya	עִירִייָה (נ)
hotel	beit malon	בֵּית מָלוֹן (ז)
bank	bank	בַּנק (ז)
embassy	ʃagrirut	שַׁגרִירוּת (נ)
travel agency	soxnut nesi'ot	סוֹכנוּת נְסִיעוֹת (נ)
information office	modi'in	מוֹדִיעִין (ז)
currency exchange	misrad hamarat mat'be'a	מִשׂרַד הֲמָרַת מַטבֵּעַ (ז)
subway	ra'kevet taxtit	רַכֶּבֶת תַחתִית (נ)
hospital	beit xolim	בֵּית חוֹלִים (ז)
gas station	taxanat 'delek	תַחֲנַת דֶלֶק (נ)
parking lot	migraʃ xanaya	מִגרָשׁ חֲנָיָה (ז)

55. Signs

signboard (store sign, etc.)	'ʃelet	שֶׁלֶט (ז)
notice (door sign, etc.)	moda'a	מוֹדָעָה (נ)
poster	'poster	פּוֹסְטֶר (ז)
direction sign	tamrur	תַּמְרוּר (ז)
arrow (sign)	χets	חֵץ (ז)
caution	azhara	אַזְהָרָה (נ)
warning sign	'ʃelet azhara	שֶׁלֶט אַזְהָרָה (ז)
to warn (vt)	lehazhir	לְהַזְהִיר
rest day (weekly ~)	yom 'χofeʃ	יוֹם חוֹפֶשׁ (ז)
timetable (schedule)	'luaχ zmanim	לוּחַ זְמַנִּים (ז)
opening hours	ʃa'ot avoda	שְׁעוֹת עֲבוֹדָה (נ"ר)
WELCOME!	bruχim haba'im!	בְּרוּכִים הַבָּאִים!
ENTRANCE	knisa	כְּנִיסָה
EXIT	yetsi'a	יְצִיאָה
PUSH	dχof	דְחוֹף
PULL	mʃoχ	מְשׁוֹך
OPEN	pa'tuaχ	פָּתוּחַ
CLOSED	sagur	סָגוּר
WOMEN	lenaʃim	לְנָשִׁים
MEN	legvarim	לִגְבָרִים
DISCOUNTS	hanaχot	הֲנָחוֹת
SALE	mivtsa	מִבְצָע
NEW!	χadaʃ!	חָדָשׁ!
FREE	χinam	חִינָם
ATTENTION!	sim lev!	שִׂים לֵב!
NO VACANCIES	ein makom panui	אֵין מָקוֹם פָּנוּי
RESERVED	ʃamur	שָׁמוּר
ADMINISTRATION	hanhala	הַנְהָלָה
STAFF ONLY	le'ovdim bilvad	לְעוֹבְדִים בִּלְבַד
BEWARE OF THE DOG!	zehirut 'kelev noʃeχ!	זְהִירוּת, כֶּלֶב נוֹשֵׁךְ!
NO SMOKING	asur le'aʃen!	אָסוּר לְעַשֵׁן!
DO NOT TOUCH!	lo lagaat!	לֹא לָגַעַת!
DANGEROUS	mesukan	מְסוּכָּן
DANGER	sakana	סַכָּנָה
HIGH VOLTAGE	'metaχ ga'voha	מֶתַח גָּבוֹהַּ
NO SWIMMING!	haraχatsa asura!	הָרַחָצָה אֲסוּרָה!
OUT OF ORDER	lo oved	לֹא עוֹבֵד
FLAMMABLE	dalik	דָלִיק
FORBIDDEN	asur	אָסוּר

NO TRESPASSING!	asur la'avor	אָסוּר לַעֲבוֹר
WET PAINT	'tseva laҳ	צֶבַע לַח

56. Urban transportation

bus	'otobus	אוֹטוֹבּוּס (ז)
streetcar	ra'kevet kala	רַכֶּבֶת קַלָה (נ)
trolley bus	tro'leibus	טרוֹלֵיבּוּס (ז)
route (of bus, etc.)	maslul	מַסלוּל (ז)
number (e.g., bus ~)	mispar	מִספָּר (ז)
to go by ...	lin'so'a be...	לִנסוֹעַ בְּ...
to get on (~ the bus)	la'alot	לַעֲלוֹת
to get off ...	la'redet mi...	לָרֶדֶת מִ...
stop (e.g., bus ~)	taҳana	תַחֲנָה (נ)
next stop	hataҳana haba'a	הַתַחֲנָה הַבָּאָה (נ)
terminus	hataҳana ha'aҳrona	הַתַחֲנָה הָאַחֲרוֹנָה (נ)
schedule	'luaҳ zmanim	לוּחַ זמַנִים (ז)
to wait (vt)	lehamtin	לְהַמתִין
ticket	kartis	כַּרטִיס (ז)
fare	meҳir hanesiya	מְחִיר הַנְסִיעָה (ז)
cashier (ticket seller)	kupai	קוּפַּאי (ז)
ticket inspection	bi'koret kartisim	בִּיקוֹרֶת כַּרטִיסִים (נ)
ticket inspector	mevaker	מְבַקֵר (ז)
to be late (for ...)	le'aҳer	לְאַחֵר
to miss (~ the train, etc.)	lefasfes	לְפַספֵס
to be in a hurry	lemaher	לְמַהֵר
taxi, cab	monit	מוֹנִית (נ)
taxi driver	nahag monit	נַהַג מוֹנִית (ז)
by taxi	bemonit	בְּמוֹנִית
taxi stand	taҳanat moniyot	תַחֲנַת מוֹנִיוֹת (נ)
to call a taxi	lehazmin monit	לְהַזמִין מוֹנִית
to take a taxi	la'kaҳat monit	לָקַחַת מוֹנִית
traffic	tnu'a	תנוּעָה (נ)
traffic jam	pkak	פּקָק (ז)
rush hour	ʃa'ot 'omes	שְׁעוֹת עוֹמֶס (נ״ר)
to park (vi)	laҳanot	לַחֲנוֹת
to park (vt)	lehaҳnot	לְהַחנוֹת
parking lot	ҳanaya	חֲנָיָה (נ)
subway	ra'kevet taҳtit	רַכֶּבֶת תַחתִית (נ)
station	taҳana	תַחֲנָה (נ)
to take the subway	lin'so'a betaҳtit	לִנסוֹעַ בְּתַחתִית
train	ra'kevet	רַכֶּבֶת (נ)
train station	taҳanat ra'kevet	תַחֲנַת רַכֶּבֶת (נ)

57. Sightseeing

monument	an'darta	אַנְדַּרְטָה (נ)
fortress	mivtsar	מִבְצָר (ז)
palace	armon	אַרְמוֹן (ז)
castle	tira	טִירָה (נ)
tower	migdal	מִגְדָּל (ז)
mausoleum	ma'uzo'le'um	מָאוּזוֹלְיאוּם (ז)
architecture	adrixalut	אַדְרִיכָלוּת (נ)
medieval (adj)	benaimi	בֵּינַיימִי
ancient (adj)	atik	עָתִיק
national (adj)	le'umi	לְאוּמִי
famous (monument, etc.)	mefursam	מְפוּרְסָם
tourist	tayar	תַּייָר (ז)
guide (person)	madrix tiyulim	מַדְרִיךְ טִיוּלִים (ז)
excursion, sightseeing tour	tiyul	טִיוּל (ז)
to show (vt)	lehar'ot	לְהַרְאוֹת
to tell (vt)	lesaper	לְסַפֵּר
to find (vt)	limtso	לִמְצוֹא
to get lost (lose one's way)	la'lexet le'ibud	לָלֶכֶת לְאִיבּוּד
map (e.g., subway ~)	mapa	מַפָּה (נ)
map (e.g., city ~)	tarʃim	תַּרְשִׁים (ז)
souvenir, gift	maz'keret	מַזְכֶּרֶת (נ)
gift shop	xanut matanot	חֲנוּת מַתָּנוֹת (נ)
to take pictures	letsalem	לְצַלֵּם
to have one's picture taken	lehitstalem	לְהִצְטַלֵּם

58. Shopping

to buy (purchase)	liknot	לִקְנוֹת
purchase	kniya	קְנִייָה (נ)
to go shopping	la'lexet lekniyot	לָלֶכֶת לִקְנִיוֹת
shopping	arixat kniyot	עֲרִיכַת קְנִיוֹת (נ)
to be open (ab. store)	pa'tuax	פָּתוּחַ
to be closed	sagur	סָגוּר
footwear, shoes	na'a'layim	נַעֲלַיים (נ״ר)
clothes, clothing	bgadim	בְּגָדִים (ז״ר)
cosmetics	tamrukim	תַּמְרוּקִים (ז״ר)
food products	mutsrei mazon	מוּצְרֵי מָזוֹן (ז״ר)
gift, present	matana	מַתָּנָה (נ)
salesman	moxer	מוֹכֵר (ז)
saleswoman	mo'xeret	מוֹכֶרֶת (נ)

check out, cash desk	kupa	קוּפָּה (נ)
mirror	mar'a	מַרְאָה (נ)
counter (store ~)	duxan	דּוּכָן (ז)
fitting room	'xeder halbaʃa	חֲדַר הַלבָּשָׁה (ז)
to try on	limdod	לִמדוֹד
to fit (ab. dress, etc.)	lehat'im	לְהַתאִים
to like (I like …)	limtso xen be'ei'nayim	לִמצוֹא חֵן בָּעֵינַיִים
price	mexir	מְחִיר (ז)
price tag	tag mexir	תַג מְחִיר (ז)
to cost (vt)	la'alot	לַעֲלוֹת
How much?	'kama	כַּמָה?
discount	hanaxa	הֲנָחָה (נ)
inexpensive (adj)	lo yakar	לֹא יָקָר
cheap (adj)	zol	זוֹל
expensive (adj)	yakar	יָקָר
It's expensive	ze yakar	זֶה יָקָר
rental (n)	haskara	הַשֹכָּרָה (נ)
to rent (~ a tuxedo)	liskor	לִשֹכּוֹר
credit (trade credit)	aʃrai	אַשׁרַאי (ז)
on credit (adv)	be'aʃrai	בָּאַשׁרַאי

59. Money

money	'kesef	כֶּסֶף (ז)
currency exchange	hamara	הֲמָרָה (נ)
exchange rate	'ʃa'ar xalifin	שַׁעַר חֲלִיפִין (ז)
ATM	kaspomat	כַּספּוֹמָט (ז)
coin	mat'be'a	מַטבֵּעַ (ז)
dollar	'dolar	דוֹלָר (ז)
euro	'eiro	אֵירוֹ (ז)
lira	'lira	לִירָה (נ)
Deutschmark	mark germani	מַרק גֶרמָנִי (ז)
franc	frank	פרַנק (ז)
pound sterling	'lira 'sterling	לִירָה שׁטֶרלִינג (נ)
yen	yen	יֶן (ז)
debt	xov	חוֹב (ז)
debtor	'ba'al xov	בַּעַל חוֹב (ז)
to lend (money)	lehalvot	לְהַלווֹת
to borrow (vi, vt)	lilvot	לִלווֹת
bank	bank	בַּנק (ז)
account	xeʃbon	חֶשׁבּוֹן (ז)
to deposit (vt)	lehafkid	לְהַפקִיד

| to deposit into the account | lehafkid leχeʃbon | לְהַפְקִיד לְחֶשְׁבּוֹן |
| to withdraw (vt) | limʃoχ meχeʃbon | לִמְשׁוֹך מֵחֶשְׁבּוֹן |

credit card	kartis aʃrai	כַּרְטִיס אַשְׁרַאי (ז)
cash	mezuman	מְזוּמָן
check	tʃek	צֶ׳ק (ז)
to write a check	liχtov tʃek	לִכְתוֹב צֶ׳ק
checkbook	pinkas 'tʃekim	פִּנְקַס צֶ׳קִים (ז)

wallet	arnak	אַרְנָק (ז)
change purse	arnak lematbe''ot	אַרְנָק לְמַטְבְּעוֹת (ז)
safe	ka'sefet	כַּסֶפֶת (נ)

heir	yoreʃ	יוֹרֵשׁ (ז)
inheritance	yeruʃa	יְרוּשָׁה (נ)
fortune (wealth)	'oʃer	עוֹשֶׁר (ז)

lease	χoze sχirut	חוֹזֶה שְׂכִירוּת (ז)
rent (money)	sχar dira	שְׂכַר דִירָה (ז)
to rent (sth from sb)	liskor	לִשְׂכּוֹר

price	meχir	מְחִיר (ז)
cost	alut	עָלוּת (נ)
sum	sχum	סְכוּם (ז)

to spend (vt)	lehotsi	לְהוֹצִיא
expenses	hotsa'ot	הוֹצָאוֹת (נ"ר)
to economize (vi, vt)	laχasoχ	לַחֲסוֹך
economical	χesχoni	חֶסְכוֹנִי

to pay (vi, vt)	leʃalem	לְשַׁלֵם
payment	taʃlum	תַשְׁלוּם (ז)
change (give the ~)	'odef	עוֹדֶף (ז)

tax	mas	מַס (ז)
fine	knas	קְנָס (ז)
to fine (vt)	liknos	לִקְנוֹס

60. Post. Postal service

post office	'do'ar	דוֹאַר (ז)
mail (letters, etc.)	'do'ar	דוֹאַר (ז)
mailman	davar	דַוָור (ז)
opening hours	ʃa'ot avoda	שְׁעוֹת עֲבוֹדָה (נ"ר)

letter	miχtav	מִכְתָב (ז)
registered letter	miχtav raʃum	מִכְתָב רָשׁוּם (ז)
postcard	gluya	גלוּיָה (נ)
telegram	mivrak	מִבְרָק (ז)
package (parcel)	χavila	חֲבִילָה (נ)

money transfer	ha'avarat ksafim	הַעֲבָרַת כְּסָפִים (נ)
to receive (vt)	lekabel	לְקַבֵּל
to send (vt)	liʃ'loaχ	לִשְׁלוֹחַ
sending	ʃliχa	שְׁלִיחָה (נ)
address	'ktovet	כְּתוֹבֶת (נ)
ZIP code	mikud	מִיקוּד (ז)
sender	ʃo'leaχ	שׁוֹלֵחַ (ז)
receiver	nim'an	נִמְעָן (ז)
name (first name)	ʃem prati	שֵׁם פְּרָטִי (ז)
surname (last name)	ʃem miʃpaχa	שֵׁם מִשְׁפָּחָה (ז)
postage rate	ta'arif	תַּעֲרִיף (ז)
standard (adj)	ragil	רָגִיל
economical (adj)	χesχoni	חֶסְכוֹנִי
weight	miʃkal	מִשְׁקָל (ז)
to weigh (~ letters)	liʃkol	לִשְׁקוֹל
envelope	ma'atafa	מַעֲטָפָה (נ)
postage stamp	bul 'do'ar	בּוּל דּוֹאַר (ז)
to stamp an envelope	lehadbik bul	לְהַדְבִּיק בּוּל

Dwelling. House. Home

61. House. Electricity

electricity	χaʃmal	חַשְׁמַל (ז)
light bulb	nura	נוּרָה (נ)
switch	'meteg	מֶתֶג (ז)
fuse (plug fuse)	natiχ	נָתִיך (ז)
cable, wire (electric ~)	χut	חוּט (ז)
wiring	χivut	חִיווּט (ז)
electricity meter	mone χaʃmal	מוֹנֶה חַשְׁמַל (ז)
readings	kri'a	קְרִיאָה (נ)

62. Villa. Mansion

country house	'bayit bakfar	בַּיִת בַּכְּפָר (ז)
villa (seaside ~)	'vila	וִילָה (נ)
wing (~ of a building)	agaf	אָגַף (ז)
garden	gan	גַן (ז)
park	park	פַּארק (ז)
tropical greenhouse	χamama	חָמָמָה (נ)
to look after (garden, etc.)	legadel	לְגַדֵל
swimming pool	breχat sχiya	בְּרֵיכַת שְׂחִייָה (נ)
gym (home gym)	'χeder 'koʃer	חָדָר כּוֹשֶר (ז)
tennis court	migraʃ 'tenis	מִגרַש טָנִיס (ז)
home theater (room)	'χeder hakrana beiti	חָדָר הַקְרָנָה בֵּיתִי (ז)
garage	musaχ	מוּסָך (ז)
private property	reχuʃ prati	רְכוּש פְּרָטִי (ז)
private land	'ʃetaχ prati	שֶטַח פְּרָטִי (ז)
warning (caution)	azhara	אַזהָרָה (נ)
warning sign	'ʃelet azhara	שֶלֶט אַזהָרָה (ז)
security	avtaχa	אַבטָחָה (נ)
security guard	ʃomer	שוֹמֵר (ז)
burglar alarm	ma'a'reχet az'aka	מַעֲרֶכֶת אַזעָקָה (נ)

63. Apartment

apartment	dira	דִירָה (נ)
room	'xeder	חֶדֶר (ז)
bedroom	xadar ʃena	חָדַר שֵׁינָה (ז)
dining room	pinat 'oxel	פִּינַת אוֹכֶל (נ)
living room	salon	סָלוֹן (ז)
study (home office)	xadar avoda	חָדַר עָבוֹדָה (ז)
entry room	prozdor	פרוֹזדוֹר (ז)
bathroom (room with a bath or shower)	xadar am'batya	חָדַר אַמבַּטיָה (ז)
half bath	ʃerutim	שֵירוּתִים (ז"ר)
ceiling	tikra	תִקרָה (נ)
floor	ritspa	רִצפָּה (נ)
corner	pina	פִּינָה (נ)

64. Furniture. Interior

furniture	rehitim	רָהִיטִים (ז"ר)
table	ʃulxan	שוּלחָן (ז)
chair	kise	כִּסֵא (ז)
bed	mita	מִיטָה (נ)
couch, sofa	sapa	סַפָּה (נ)
armchair	kursa	כּוּרסָה (נ)
bookcase	aron sfarim	אֲרוֹן ספָרִים (ז)
shelf	madaf	מַדָף (ז)
wardrobe	aron bgadim	אֲרוֹן בּגָדִים (ז)
coat rack (wall-mounted ~)	mitle	מִתלֶה (ז)
coat stand	mitle	מִתלֶה (ז)
bureau, dresser	ʃida	שִידָה (נ)
coffee table	ʃulxan itonim	שוּלחַן עִיתוֹנִים (ז)
mirror	mar'a	מַראָה (נ)
carpet	ʃa'tiax	שָטִיחַ (ז)
rug, small carpet	ʃa'tiax	שָטִיחַ (ז)
fireplace	ax	אָח (נ)
candle	ner	נֵר (ז)
candlestick	pamot	פָּמוֹט (ז)
drapes	vilonot	וִילוֹנוֹת (ז"ר)
wallpaper	tapet	טַפֶּט (ז)
blinds (jalousie)	trisim	תרִיסִים (ז"ר)
table lamp	menorat ʃulxan	מְנוֹרַת שוּלחָן (נ)

wall lamp (sconce)	menorat kir	מְנוֹרַת קִיר (נ)
floor lamp	menora o'medet	מְנוֹרָה עוֹמֶדֶת (נ)
chandelier	niv'reʃet	נִבְרֶשֶׁת (נ)
leg (of chair, table)	'regel	רֶגֶל (נ)
armrest	miʃ'enet yad	מִשְׁעֶנֶת יָד (נ)
back (backrest)	miʃ'enet	מִשְׁעֶנֶת (נ)
drawer	megera	מְגֵירָה (נ)

65. Bedding

bedclothes	matsa'im	מַצָּעִים (ז"ר)
pillow	karit	כָּרִית (נ)
pillowcase	tsipit	צִיפִּית (נ)
duvet, comforter	smiχa	שְׂמִיכָה (נ)
sheet	sadin	סָדִין (ז)
bedspread	kisui mita	כִּיסוּי מִיטָה (ז)

66. Kitchen

kitchen	mitbaχ	מִטְבָּח (ז)
gas	gaz	גָז (ז)
gas stove (range)	tanur gaz	תַּנוּר גָז (ז)
electric stove	tanur χaʃmali	תַּנוּר חַשְׁמַלִי (ז)
oven	tanur afiya	תַּנוּר אֲפִיָה (ז)
microwave oven	mikrogal	מִיקרוֹגַל (ז)
refrigerator	mekarer	מְקָרֵר (ז)
freezer	makpi	מַקְפִּיא (ז)
dishwasher	me'diaχ kelim	מֵדִיחַ כֵּלִים (ז)
meat grinder	matχenat basar	מַטְחֵנַת בָּשָׂר (נ)
juicer	masχeta	מַסְחֵטָה (נ)
toaster	'toster	טוֹסְטֵר (ז)
mixer	'mikser	מִיקְסֵר (ז)
coffee machine	meχonat kafe	מְכוֹנַת קָפֶה (נ)
coffee pot	findʒan	פִינְגַ׳אן (ז)
coffee grinder	matχenat kafe	מַטְחֵנַת קָפֶה (נ)
kettle	kumkum	קוּמְקוּם (ז)
teapot	kumkum	קוּמְקוּם (ז)
lid	miχse	מִכְסֶה (ז)
tea strainer	mis'nenet te	מְסַנֶנֶת תֵה (נ)
spoon	kaf	כַּף (נ)
teaspoon	kapit	כַּפִּית (נ)
soup spoon	kaf	כַּף (נ)

fork	mazleg	מַזְלֵג (ז)
knife	sakin	סַכִּין (ז, נ)
tableware (dishes)	kelim	כֵּלִים (ז״ר)
plate (dinner ~)	tsa'laxat	צַלַחַת (נ)
saucer	taxtit	תַחְתִית (נ)
shot glass	kosit	כּוֹסִית (נ)
glass (tumbler)	kos	כּוֹס (נ)
cup	'sefel	סֵפֶל (ז)
sugar bowl	mis'keret	מִסְכֶּרֶת (נ)
salt shaker	milxiya	מִלְחִיָה (נ)
pepper shaker	pilpeliya	פִּלְפְּלִיָה (נ)
butter dish	maxame'a	מַחֲמָאָה (נ)
stock pot (soup pot)	sir	סִיר (ז)
frying pan (skillet)	maxvat	מַחֲבַת (נ)
ladle	tarvad	תַרְוָד (ז)
colander	mis'nenet	מְסַנֶּנֶת (נ)
tray (serving ~)	magaʃ	מַגָשׁ (ז)
bottle	bakbuk	בַּקְבּוּק (ז)
jar (glass)	tsin'tsenet	צִנְצֶנֶת (נ)
can	paxit	פַּחִית (נ)
bottle opener	potxan bakbukim	פּוֹתְחָן בַּקְבּוּקִים (ז)
can opener	potxan kufsa'ot	פּוֹתְחָן קוּפְסָאוֹת (ז)
corkscrew	maxlets	מַחְלֵץ (ז)
filter	'filter	פִילְטֶר (ז)
to filter (vt)	lesanen	לְסַנֵן
trash, garbage (food waste, etc.)	'zevel	זֶבֶל (ז)
trash can (kitchen ~)	pax 'zevel	פַּח זֶבֶל (ז)

67. Bathroom

bathroom	xadar am'batya	חֲדַר אַמְבַּטְיָה (ז)
water	'mayim	מַיִם (ז״ר)
faucet	'berez	בֶּרֶז (ז)
hot water	'mayim xamim	מַיִם חַמִים (ז״ר)
cold water	'mayim karim	מַיִם קָרִים (ז״ר)
toothpaste	mifxat ʃi'nayim	מִשְׁחַת שִׁינַיִים (נ)
to brush one's teeth	letsax'tseax ʃi'nayim	לְצַחְצֵחַ שִׁינַיִים
toothbrush	miv'reʃet ʃi'nayim	מִבְרֶשֶׁת שִׁינַיִים (נ)
to shave (vi)	lehitga'leax	לְהִתְגַלֵחַ
shaving foam	'ketsef gi'luax	קֶצֶף גִילוּחַ (ז)

razor	'ta'ar	תַּעַר (ז)
to wash (one's hands, etc.)	liſtof	לִשְׁטוֹף
to take a bath	lehitraxets	לְהִתְרַחֵץ
shower	mik'laxat	מִקְלַחַת (נ)
to take a shower	lehitka'leax	לְהִתְקַלֵּחַ
bathtub	am'batya	אַמְבַּטְיָה (נ)
toilet (toilet bowl)	asla	אַסְלָה (נ)
sink (washbasin)	kiyor	כִּיּוֹר (ז)
soap	sabon	סַבּוֹן (ז)
soap dish	saboniya	סַבּוֹנִיָּה (נ)
sponge	sfog 'lifa	סְפוֹג לִיפָה (ז)
shampoo	ʃampu	שַׁמְפּוּ (ז)
towel	ma'gevet	מַגֶּבֶת (נ)
bathrobe	xaluk raxatsa	חָלוּק רַחְצָה (ז)
laundry (process)	kvisa	כְּבִיסָה (נ)
washing machine	mexonat kvisa	מְכוֹנַת כְּבִיסָה (נ)
to do the laundry	lexabes	לְכַבֵּס
laundry detergent	avkat kvisa	אַבְקַת כְּבִיסָה (נ)

68. Household appliances

TV set	tele'vizya	טֶלֶוִוִיזְיָה (נ)
tape recorder	teip	טֵייפּ (ז)
VCR (video recorder)	maxʃir 'vide'o	מַכְשִׁיר וִידָאוֹ (ז)
radio	'radyo	רַדְיוֹ (ז)
player (CD, MP3, etc.)	nagan	נַגָּן (ז)
video projector	makren	מַקְרֵן (ז)
home movie theater	kol'no'a beiti	קוֹלְנוֹעַ בֵּיתִי (ז)
DVD player	nagan dividi	נַגָּן DVD (ז)
amplifier	magber	מַגְבֵּר (ז)
video game console	maxʃir plei'steiʃen	מַכְשִׁיר פְּלֵייסְטֵיישֶׁן (ז)
video camera	matslemat 'vide'o	מַצְלֵמַת וִידָאוֹ (נ)
camera (photo)	matslema	מַצְלֵמָה (נ)
digital camera	matslema digi'talit	מַצְלֵמָה דִיגִיטָלִית (נ)
vacuum cleaner	ʃo'ev avak	שׁוֹאֵב אָבָק (ז)
iron (e.g., steam ~)	maghets	מַגְהֵץ (ז)
ironing board	'kereʃ gihuts	קֶרֶשׁ גִּיהוּץ (ז)
telephone	'telefon	טֶלֶפוֹן (ז)
cell phone	'telefon nayad	טֶלֶפוֹן נַיָּיד (ז)
typewriter	mexonat ktiva	מְכוֹנַת כְּתִיבָה (נ)
sewing machine	mexonat tfira	מְכוֹנַת תְּפִירָה (נ)
microphone	mikrofon	מִיקְרוֹפוֹן (ז)

headphones	ozniyot	אוֹזְנִיּוֹת (נ״ר)
remote control (TV)	'ʃelet	שֶׁלֶט (ז)
CD, compact disc	taklitor	תַקְלִיטוֹר (ז)
cassette, tape	ka'letet	קַלֶּטֶת (נ)
vinyl record	taklit	תַקְלִיט (ז)

HUMAN ACTIVITIES

Job. Business. Part 1

69. Office. Working in the office

office (company ~)	misrad	מִשׂרָד (ז)
office (of director, etc.)	misrad	מִשׂרָד (ז)
reception desk	kabala	קַבָּלָה (נ)
secretary	mazkir	מַזכִּיר (ז)
secretary (fem.)	mazkira	מַזכִּירָה (נ)
director	menahel	מְנַהֵל (ז)
manager	menahel	מְנַהֵל (ז)
accountant	menahel xeʃbonot	מְנַהֵל חָשבּוֹנוֹת (ז)
employee	oved	עוֹבֵד (ז)
furniture	rehitim	רָהִיטִים (ז״ר)
desk	ʃulxan	שׁוּלחָן (ז)
desk chair	kursa	כּוּרסָה (נ)
drawer unit	ʃidat megerot	שִׁידַת מְגֵירוֹת (נ)
coat stand	mitle	מִתלֶה (ז)
computer	maxʃev	מַחשֵׁב (ז)
printer	mad'peset	מַדפֶּסֶת (נ)
fax machine	faks	פַקס (ז)
photocopier	mexonat tsilum	מְכוֹנַת צִילוּם (נ)
paper	neyar	נְייָר (ז)
office supplies	tsiyud misradi	צִיוּד מִשׂרָדִי (ז)
mouse pad	ʃa'tiax le'axbar	שָׁטִיחַ לְעַכבָּר (ז)
sheet (of paper)	daf	דַף (ז)
binder	klaser	קלָסֵר (ז)
catalog	katalog	קָטָלוֹג (ז)
phone directory	madrix 'telefon	מַדרִיך טֶלֶפוֹן (ז)
documentation	ti'ud	תִיעוּד (ז)
brochure (e.g., 12 pages ~)	xo'veret	חוֹבֶרֶת (נ)
leaflet (promotional ~)	alon	עָלוֹן (ז)
sample	dugma	דוּגמָה (נ)
training meeting	yeʃivat hadraxa	יְשִׁיבַת הַדרָכָה (נ)
meeting (of managers)	yeʃiva	יְשִׁיבָה (נ)
lunch time	hafsakat tsaha'rayim	הַפסָקַת צָהֳרַיִים (נ)

to make a copy	letsalem mismax	לְצַלֵּם מִסמָך
to make multiple copies	lehaxin mispar otakim	לְהָכִין מִספָּר עוֹתָקִים
to receive a fax	lekabel faks	לְקַבֵּל פַקס
to send a fax	lifloax faks	לִשלוֹחַ פַקס
to call (by phone)	lehitkaʃer	לְהִתקַשֵר
to answer (vt)	la'anot	לַעֲנוֹת
to put through	lekaʃer	לְקַשֵר
to arrange, to set up	lik'bo'a pgiʃa	לִקבּוֹעַ פּגִישָה
to demonstrate (vt)	lehadgim	לְהַדגִים
to be absent	lehe'ader	לְהֵיעָדֵר
absence	he'adrut	הֵיעָדרוּת (נ)

70. Business processes. Part 1

business	'esek	עֵסֶק (ז)
occupation	isuk	עִיסוּק (ז)
firm	xevra	חֶברָה (נ)
company	xevra	חֶברָה (נ)
corporation	ta'agid	תַאֲגִיד (ז)
enterprise	'esek	עֵסֶק (ז)
agency	soxnut	סוֹכנוּת (נ)
agreement (contract)	heskem	הֶסכֵּם (ז)
contract	xoze	חוֹזֶה (ז)
deal	iska	עִסקָה (נ)
order (to place an ~)	hazmana	הַזמָנָה (נ)
terms (of the contract)	tnai	תנַאי (ז)
wholesale (adv)	besitonut	בְּסִיטוֹנוּת
wholesale (adj)	sitona'i	סִיטוֹנָאִי
wholesale (n)	sitonut	סִיטוֹנוּת (נ)
retail (adj)	kim'oni	קַמעוֹנִי
retail (n)	kim'onut	קַמעוֹנוּת (נ)
competitor	mitxare	מִתחָרֶה (ז)
competition	taxarut	תַחָרוּת (נ)
to compete (vi)	lehitxarot	לְהִתחָרוֹת
partner (associate)	ʃutaf	שוּתָף (ז)
partnership	ʃutafa	שוּתָפוּת (נ)
crisis	maʃber	מַשבֵּר (ז)
bankruptcy	pʃitat 'regel	פּשִיטַת רֶגֶל (נ)
to go bankrupt	lifʃot 'regel	לִפשוֹט רֶגֶל
difficulty	'koʃi	קוֹשִי (ז)
problem	be'aya	בְּעָיָה (נ)
catastrophe	ason	אָסוֹן (ז)
economy	kalkala	כַּלכָּלָה (נ)

economic (~ growth)	kalkali	כַּלְכָּלִי
economic recession	mitun kalkali	מִיתוּן כַּלְכָּלִי (ז)
goal (aim)	matara	מַטָרָה (נ)
task	mesima	מְשִׂימָה (נ)
to trade (vi)	lisxor	לִסְחוֹר
network (distribution ~)	'reʃet	רֶשֶׁת (נ)
inventory (stock)	maxsan	מַחְסָן (ז)
range (assortment)	mivxar	מִבְחָר (ז)
leader (leading company)	manhig	מַנְהִיג (ז)
large (~ company)	gadol	גָדוֹל
monopoly	'monopol	מוֹנוֹפּוֹל (ז)
theory	te"orya	תֵיאוֹרְיָה (נ)
practice	'praktika	פְּרַקְטִיקָה (נ)
experience (in my ~)	nisayon	נִיסָיוֹן (ז)
trend (tendency)	megama	מְגַמָה (נ)
development	pi'tuax	פִּיתוּחַ (ז)

71. Business processes. Part 2

profit (foregone ~)	'revax	רֶוַוח (ז)
profitable (~ deal)	rivxi	רִוְוחִי
delegation (group)	miʃlaxat	מִשְׁלַחַת (נ)
salary	mas'koret	מַשְׂכּוֹרֶת (נ)
to correct (an error)	letaken	לְתַקֵן
business trip	nesi'a batafkid	נְסִיעָה בַּתַפְקִיד (נ)
commission	amla	עַמְלָה (נ)
to control (vt)	liʃlot	לִשְׁלוֹט
conference	kinus	כִּינוּס (ז)
license	riʃayon	רִישָׁיוֹן (ז)
reliable (~ partner)	amin	אָמִין
initiative (undertaking)	yozma	יוֹזְמָה (נ)
norm (standard)	'norma	נוֹרְמָה (נ)
circumstance	nesibot	נְסִיבּוֹת (נ"ר)
duty (of employee)	xova	חוֹבָה (נ)
organization (company)	irgun	אִרגוּן (ז)
organization (process)	hit'argenut	הִתְאַרְגְנוּת (נ)
organized (adj)	me'urgan	מְאוּרְגָן
cancellation	bitul	בִּיטוּל (ז)
to cancel (call off)	levatel	לְבַטֵל
report (official ~)	dox	דוֹחַ (ז)
patent	patent	פָּטֶנט (ז)
to patent (obtain patent)	lirʃom patent	לִרְשׁוֹם פָּטֶנט

to plan (vt)	letaxnen	לְתַכְנֵן
bonus (money)	'bonus	בּוֹנוּס (ז)
professional (adj)	miktso'i	מִקְצוֹעִי
procedure	'nohal	נוֹהַל (ז)

to examine (contract, etc.)	livxon	לִבחוֹן
calculation	xiʃuv	חִישוּב (ז)
reputation	monitin	מוֹנִיטִין (ז"ר)
risk	sikun	סִיכּוּן (ז)

to manage, to run	lenahel	לְנַהֵל
information	meida	מֵידָע (ז)
property	ba'alut	בַּעֲלוּת (נ)
union	igud	אִיגוּד (ז)

life insurance	bi'tuax xayim	בִּיטוּחַ חַיִים (ז)
to insure (vt)	leva'teax	לְבַטֵחַ
insurance	bi'tuax	בִּיטוּחַ (ז)

auction (~ sale)	mexira 'pombit	מְכִירָה פּוּמבִּית (נ)
to notify (inform)	leho'dia	לְהוֹדִיעַ
management (process)	nihul	נִיהוּל (ז)
service (~ industry)	ʃirut	שֵירוּת (ז)

forum	'forum	פוֹרוּם (ז)
to function (vi)	letafked	לְתַפקֵד
stage (phase)	ʃalav	שָלָב (ז)
legal (~ services)	miʃpati	מִשפָּטִי
lawyer (legal advisor)	orex din	עוֹרֵך דִין (ז)

72. Production. Works

plant	mif'al	מִפעָל (ז)
factory	beit xa'roʃet	בֵּית חֲרוֹשֶת (ז)
workshop	agaf	אָגָף (ז)
works, production site	mif'al	מִפעָל (ז)

industry (manufacturing)	ta'asiya	תַעֲשִׂייָה (נ)
industrial (adj)	ta'asiyati	תַעֲשִׂייָתִי
heavy industry	ta'asiya kveda	תַעֲשִׂייָה כּבֵדָה (נ)
light industry	ta'asiya kala	תַעֲשִׂייָה קַלָה (נ)

products	to'tseret	תוֹצֶרֶת (נ)
to produce (vt)	leyatser	לְיַיצֵר
raw materials	'xomer 'gelem	חוֹמֶר גֶלֶם (ז)

foreman (construction ~)	menahel avoda	מְנַהֵל עֲבוֹדָה (ז)
workers team (crew)	'tsevet ovdim	צֶוֶות עוֹבדִים (ז)
worker	po'el	פּוֹעֵל (ז)
working day	yom avoda	יום עֲבוֹדָה (ז)

pause (rest break)	hafsaka	הַפְסָקָה (נ)
meeting	yeʃiva	יְשִׁיבָה (נ)
to discuss (vt)	ladun	לָדוּן

plan	toxnit	תוֹכְנִית (נ)
to fulfill the plan	leva'tse'a et hatoxnit	לְבַצֵּעַ אֶת הַתוֹכְנִית
rate of output	'ketsev tfuka	קֶצֶב תְפוּקָה (ז)
quality	eixut	אֵיכוּת (נ)
control (checking)	bakara	בַּקָרָה (נ)
quality control	bakarat eixut	בַּקָרַת אֵיכוּת (נ)

workplace safety	betixut beavoda	בְּטִיחוּת בָּעֲבוֹדָה (נ)
discipline	miʃma'at	מִשְׁמַעַת (נ)
violation	hafara	הֲפָרָה (נ)
(of safety rules, etc.)		
to violate (rules)	lehafer	לְהָפֵר

strike	ʃvita	שְׁבִיתָה (נ)
striker	ʃovet	שׁוֹבֵת (ז)
to be on strike	liʃbot	לִשְׁבּוֹת
labor union	igud ovdim	אִיגוּד עוֹבְדִים (ז)

to invent (machine, etc.)	lehamtsi	לְהַמְצִיא
invention	hamtsa'a	הַמְצָאָה (נ)
research	mexkar	מֶחְקָר (ז)
to improve (make better)	leʃaper	לְשַׁפֵּר

| technology | texno'logya | טֶכְנוֹלוֹגְיָה (נ) |
| technical drawing | sirtut | שִׂרטוּט (ז) |

load, cargo	mit'an	מִטעָן (ז)
loader (person)	sabal	סַבָּל (ז)
to load (vehicle, etc.)	leha'amis	לְהַעֲמִיס
loading (process)	ha'amasa	הַעֲמָסָה (נ)

| to unload (vi, vt) | lifrok mit'an | לִפרוֹק מִטעָן |
| unloading | prika | פְּרִיקָה (נ) |

transportation	hovala	הוֹבָלָה (נ)
transportation company	xevrat hovala	חֶבְרַת הוֹבָלָה (נ)
to transport (vt)	lehovil	לְהוֹבִיל

freight car	karon	קָרוֹן (ז)
tank (e.g., oil ~)	mexalit	מֵיכָלִית (נ)
truck	masa'it	מַשָׂאִית (נ)

| machine tool | mexonat ibud | מְכוֹנַת עִיבּוּד (נ) |
| mechanism | manganon | מַנגָנוֹן (ז) |

industrial waste	'psolet ta'asiyatit	פְּסוֹלֶת תַעֲשִׂייָתִית (נ)
packing (process)	ariza	אֲרִיזָה (נ)
to pack (vt)	le'eroz	לֶאֱרוֹז

73. Contract. Agreement

contract	xoze	חוֹזֶה (ז)
agreement	heskem	הֶסכֵּם (ז)
addendum	'sefax	סֶפַח (ז)
to sign a contract	la'arox heskem	לַעֲרוֹך הֶסכֵּם
signature	xatima	חֲתִימָה (נ)
to sign (vt)	laxtom	לַחתוֹם
seal (stamp)	xo'temet	חוֹתֶמֶת (נ)
subject of contract	nose haxoze	נוֹשֵׂא הַחוֹזֶה (ז)
clause	se'if	סָעִיף (ז)
parties (in contract)	tsdadim	צְדָדִים (ז"ר)
legal address	'ktovet miʃpatit	כְּתוֹבֶת מִשפָּטִית (נ)
to violate the contract	lehafer xoze	לְהָפֵר חוֹזֶה
commitment (obligation)	hitxaivut	הִתחַייבוּת (נ)
responsibility	axrayut	אַחרָיוּת (נ)
force majeure	'koax elyon	כּוֹחַ עֶליוֹן (ז)
dispute	vi'kuax	וִיכּוּחַ (ז)
penalties	itsumim	עִיצוּמִים (ז"ר)

74. Import & Export

import	ye'vu'a	יְבוּא (ז)
importer	yevu'an	יְבוּאָן (ז)
to import (vt)	leyabe	לְייַבֵּא
import (as adj.)	meyuba	מְיוּבָּא
export (exportation)	yitsu	יְיצוּא (ז)
exporter	yetsu'an	יְצוּאָן (ז)
to export (vi, vt)	leyatse	לְייַצֵא
export (as adj.)	ʃel yitsu	שֶל יְיצוּא
goods (merchandise)	sxora	סחוֹרָה (נ)
consignment, lot	miʃ'loax	מִשלוֹחַ (ז)
weight	miʃkal	מִשקָל (ז)
volume	'nefax	נֶפַח (ז)
cubic meter	'meter me'ukav	מֶטֶר מְעוּקָב (ז)
manufacturer	yatsran	יַצרָן (ז)
transportation company	xevrat hovala	חֶברַת הוֹבָלָה (נ)
container	mexula	מְכוּלָה (נ)
border	gvul	גְבוּל (ז)
customs	'mexes	מֶכֶס (ז)
customs duty	mas 'mexes	מַס מֶכֶס (ז)

customs officer	pakid 'meχes	פָּקִיד מֶכֶס (ז)
smuggling	havraχa	הַבְרָחָה (נ)
contraband (smuggled goods)	sχora muv'reχet	סחוֹרָה מובְרַחַת (נ)

75. Finances

stock (share)	menaya	מְנָיָה (נ)
bond (certificate)	i'geret χov	אִיגֶּרֶת חוֹב (נ)
promissory note	ʃtar χalifin	שטָר חֲלִיפִין (ז)

| stock exchange | 'bursa | בּוּרסָה (נ) |
| stock price | meχir hamenaya | מחִיר הַמְנָיָה (ז) |

| to go down (become cheaper) | la'redet bemeχir | לָרֶדֶת בּמְחִיר |
| to go up (become more expensive) | lehityaker | להִתיַיקֵר |

| share | menaya | מְנָיָה (נ) |
| controlling interest | ʃlita | שלִיטָה (נ) |

investment	haʃka'ot	השקָעוֹת (נ"ר)
to invest (vt)	lehaʃ'ki'a	להַשקִיעַ
percent	aχuz	אָחוּז (ז)
interest (on investment)	ribit	רִיבִּית (נ)

profit	'revaχ	רֶווַח (ז)
profitable (adj)	rivχi	רִווחִי
tax	mas	מַס (ז)

currency (foreign ~)	mat'be'a	מַטבֵּעַ (ז)
national (adj)	le'umi	לְאוּמִי
exchange (currency ~)	hamara	הַמָרָה (נ)

| accountant | ro'e χeʃbon | רוֹאֵה חֶשבּוֹן (ז) |
| accounting | hanhalat χeʃbonot | הַנהָלַת חָשבּוֹנוֹת (נ) |

bankruptcy	pʃitat 'regel	פּשִיטַת רֶגֶל (נ)
collapse, crash	krisa	קרִיסָה (נ)
ruin	pʃitat 'regel	פּשִיטַת רֶגֶל (נ)
to be ruined (financially)	lifʃot 'regel	לִפשוֹט רֶגֶל
inflation	inf'latsya	אִינפלַציָה (נ)
devaluation	piχut	פִּיחוּת (ז)

capital	hon	הוֹן (ז)
income	haχnasa	הַכנָסָה (נ)
turnover	maχzor	מַחזוֹר (ז)
resources	maʃabim	מַשאַבִּים (ז"ר)
monetary resources	emtsa'im kaspiyim	אֶמצָעִים כַּספִּיִים (ז"ר)

overhead	hotsa'ot	הוֹצָאוֹת (נ״ר)
to reduce (expenses)	letsamtsem	לְצַמְצֵם

76. Marketing

marketing	ʃivuk	שִׁיווּק (ז)
market	ʃuk	שׁוּק (ז)
market segment	'pelaχ ʃuk	פֶּלַח שׁוּק (ז)
product	mutsar	מוּצָר (ז)
goods (merchandise)	sχora	סְחוֹרָה (נ)
brand	mutag	מוּתָג (ז)
trademark	'semel misχari	סֶמֶל מִסְחָרִי (ז)
logotype	'semel haχevra	סֶמֶל הַחֶבְרָה (ז)
logo	'logo	לוֹגוֹ (ז)
demand	bikuʃ	בִּיקוּשׁ (ז)
supply	he'tse'a	הֶיצֵעַ (ז)
need	'tsoreχ	צוֹרֶךְ (ז)
consumer	tsarχan	צַרְכָן (ז)
analysis	ni'tuaχ	נִיתוּחַ (ז)
to analyze (vt)	lena'teaχ	לְנַתֵחַ
positioning	mitsuv	מִיצוּב (ז)
to position (vt)	lematsev	לְמַצֵב
price	meχir	מְחִיר (ז)
pricing policy	mediniyut timχur	מְדִינִיוּת תַמְחוּר (נ)
price formation	hamχara	הַמְחָרָה (נ)

77. Advertising

advertising	pirsum	פִּרְסוּם (ז)
to advertise (vt)	lefarsem	לְפַרְסֵם
budget	taktsiv	תַקְצִיב (ז)
ad, advertisement	pir'somet	פִּרְסוֹמֶת (נ)
TV advertising	pir'somet tele'vizya	פִּרְסוֹמֶת טֶלֶווִיזְיָה (נ)
radio advertising	pir'somet 'radyo	פִּרְסוֹמֶת רַדְיוֹ (נ)
outdoor advertising	pirsum χutsot	פִּרְסוּם חוּצוֹת (ז)
mass media	emtsa'ei tik'ʃoret hamonim	אֶמְצָעֵי תִקְשׁוֹרֶת הַמוֹנִים (ז״ר)
periodical (n)	ktav et	כְּתַב עֵת (ז)
image (public appearance)	tadmit	תַדְמִית (נ)
slogan	sisma	סִיסְמָה (נ)
motto (maxim)	'moto	מוֹטוֹ (ז)
campaign	masa	מַסָע (ז)

advertising campaign	masa pirsum	מַסָע פִּרְסוּם (ז)
target group	oxlusiyat 'ya'ad	אוֹכְלוּסִייַת יַעַד (נ)
business card	kartis bikur	כַּרְטִיס בִּיקוּר (ז)
leaflet (promotional ~)	alon	עָלוֹן (ז)
brochure (e.g., 12 pages ~)	xo'veret	חוֹבֶרֶת (נ)
pamphlet	alon	עָלוֹן (ז)
newsletter	alon meida	עָלוֹן מֵידָע (ז)
signboard (store sign, etc.)	'ʃelet	שֶׁלֶט (ז)
poster	'poster	פּוֹסטֶר (ז)
billboard	'luax pirsum	לוּחַ פִּרְסוּם (ז)

78. Banking

bank	bank	בַּנק (ז)
branch (of bank, etc.)	snif	סנִיף (ז)
bank clerk, consultant	yo'ets	יוֹעֵץ (ז)
manager (director)	menahel	מְנַהֵל (ז)
bank account	xeʃbon	חֶשבּוֹן (ז)
account number	mispar xeʃbon	מִספַּר חֶשבּוֹן (ז)
checking account	xeʃbon over vaʃav	חֶשבּוֹן עוֹבֵר וָשָב (ז)
savings account	xeʃbon xisaxon	חֶשבּוֹן חִסָכוֹן (ז)
to open an account	lif'toax xeʃbon	לִפתוֹחַ חֶשבּוֹן
to close the account	lisgor xeʃbon	לִסגוֹר חֶשבּוֹן
to deposit into the account	lehafkid lexeʃbon	לְהַפקִיד לְחֶשבּוֹן
to withdraw (vt)	limʃox mexeʃbon	לִמשוֹך מֵחֶשבּוֹן
deposit	pikadon	פִּיקָדוֹן (ז)
to make a deposit	lehafkid	לְהַפקִיד
wire transfer	ha'avara banka'it	הַעֲבָרָה בַּנקָאִית (נ)
to wire, to transfer	leha'avir 'kesef	לְהַעֲבִיר כֶּסֶף
sum	sxum	סכוּם (ז)
How much?	'kama?	כַּמָה?
signature	xatima	חֲתִימָה (נ)
to sign (vt)	laxtom	לַחתוֹם
credit card	kartis aʃrai	כַּרְטִיס אַשרַאי (ז)
code (PIN code)	kod	קוֹד (ז)
credit card number	mispar kartis aʃrai	מִספַּר כַּרְטִיס אַשרַאי (ז)
ATM	kaspomat	כַּספּוֹמָט (ז)
check	tʃek	צֶ'ק (ז)
to write a check	lixtov tʃek	לִכתוֹב צֶ'ק

checkbook	pinkas 'tʃekim	פִּנְקַס צֶ'קִים (ז)
loan (bank ~)	halva'a	הַלְוָאָה (נ)
to apply for a loan	levakeʃ halva'a	לְבַקֵּשׁ הַלְוָאָה
to get a loan	lekabel halva'a	לְקַבֵּל הַלְוָאָה
to give a loan	lehalvot	לְהַלְווֹת
guarantee	arvut	עָרְבוּת (נ)

79. Telephone. Phone conversation

telephone	'telefon	טֶלֶפוֹן (ז)
cell phone	'telefon nayad	טֶלֶפוֹן נַיָּיד (ז)
answering machine	meʃivon	מְשִׁיבוֹן (ז)
to call (by phone)	letsaltsel	לְצַלְצֵל
phone call	siχat 'telefon	שִׂיחַת טֶלֶפוֹן (נ)
to dial a number	leχayeg mispar	לְחַיֵּיג מִסְפָּר
Hello!	'halo!	הָלוֹ!
to ask (vt)	liʃol	לִשְׁאוֹל
to answer (vi, vt)	laʻanot	לַעֲנוֹת
to hear (vt)	liʃmoʻa	לִשְׁמוֹעַ
well (adv)	tov	טוֹב
not well (adv)	lo tov	לֹא טוֹב
noises (interference)	hafraʻot	הַפְרָעוֹת (נ"ר)
receiver	ʃfo'feret	שְׁפוֹפֶרֶת (נ)
to pick up (~ the phone)	leharim ʃfo'feret	לְהָרִים שְׁפוֹפֶרֶת
to hang up (~ the phone)	lehaʼniaχ ʃfo'feret	לְהַנִּיחַ שְׁפוֹפֶרֶת
busy (engaged)	tafus	תָּפוּס
to ring (ab. phone)	letsaltsel	לְצַלְצֵל
telephone book	'sefer tele'fonim	סֵפֶר טֶלֶפוֹנִים (ז)
local (adj)	mekomi	מְקוֹמִי
local call	siχa mekomit	שִׂיחָה מְקוֹמִית (נ)
long distance (~ call)	bein ironi	בֵּין עִירוֹנִי
long-distance call	siχa bein ironit	שִׂיחָה בֵּין עִירוֹנִית (נ)
international (adj)	benle'umi	בֵּינְלְאוּמִי
international call	siχa benle'umit	שִׂיחָה בֵּינְלְאוּמִית (נ)

80. Cell phone

cell phone	'telefon nayad	טֶלֶפוֹן נַיָּיד (ז)
display	masaχ	מָסָךְ (ז)
button	kaftor	כַּפְתּוֹר (ז)
SIM card	kartis sim	כַּרְטִיס סִים (ז)
battery	solela	סוֹלְלָה (נ)

| to be dead (battery) | lehitroken | לְהִתְרוֹקֵן |
| charger | mit'an | מִטעָן (ז) |

menu	tafrit	תַפרִיט (ז)
settings	hagdarot	הַגדָרוֹת (נ"ר)
tune (melody)	mangina	מַנגִינָה (נ)
to select (vt)	livxor	לִבחוֹר

calculator	maxʃevon	מַחשְבוֹן (ז)
voice mail	ta koli	תָא קוֹלִי (ז)
alarm clock	ʃa'on me'orer	שָעוֹן מְעוֹרֵר (ז)
contacts	anʃei 'keʃer	אַנשֵי קֶשֶר (ז"ר)

| SMS (text message) | misron | מִסרוֹן (ז) |
| subscriber | manui | מָנוּי (ז) |

81. Stationery

| ballpoint pen | et kaduri | עֵט כַּדוּרִי (ז) |
| fountain pen | et no've'a | עֵט נוֹבֵעַ (ז) |

pencil	iparon	עִיפָּרוֹן (ז)
highlighter	'marker	מַרקֵר (ז)
felt-tip pen	tuʃ	טוּש (ז)

| notepad | pinkas | פִּנקָס (ז) |
| agenda (diary) | yoman | יוֹמָן (ז) |

ruler	sargel	סַרגֵל (ז)
calculator	maxʃevon	מַחשְבוֹן (ז)
eraser	'maxak	מַחַק (ז)
thumbtack	'na'ats	נַעַץ (ז)
paper clip	mehadek	מְהַדֵק (ז)

glue	'devek	דֶבֶק (ז)
stapler	ʃadxan	שַדכָן (ז)
hole punch	menakev	מְנַקֵב (ז)
pencil sharpener	maxded	מַחדֵד (ז)

82. Kinds of business

accounting services	ʃerutei hanhalat xeʃbonot	שֵירוּתֵי הַנהָלַת חָשבּוֹנוֹת (ז"ר)
advertising	pirsum	פִּרסוּם (ז)
advertising agency	soxnut pirsum	סוֹכנוּת פִּרסוּם (נ)
air-conditioners	mazganim	מַזגָנִים (ז"ר)
airline	xevrat te'ufa	חֶברַת תְעוּפָה (נ)
alcoholic beverages	maʃka'ot xarifim	מַשקָאוֹת חָרִיפִים (נ"ר)
antiques (antique dealers)	atikot	עַתִיקוֹת (נ"ר)

art gallery (contemporary ~)	ga'lerya le'amanut	גָלֶרְיָה לְאָמָנוּת (נ)
audit services	ʃerutei bi'koret xeʃbonot	שֵירוּתֵי בִּיקוֹרֵת חָשבּוֹנוֹת (ז"ר)
banking industry	banka'ut	בַּנקָאוּת (נ)
bar	bar	בָּר (ז)
beauty parlor	mexon 'yofi	מְכוֹן יוֹפִי (ז)
bookstore	xanut sfarim	חָנוּת סְפָרִים (נ)
brewery	miv'ʃelet 'bira	מִבשֶלֶת בִּירָה (נ)
business center	merkaz asakim	מֶרכַּז עֲסָקִים (ז)
business school	beit 'sefer le'asakim	בֵּית סֵפֶר לְעֲסָקִים (ז)
casino	ka'zino	קָזִינוֹ (ז)
construction	bniya	בּנִייָה (נ)
consulting	yi'uts	יִיעוּץ (ז)
dental clinic	mirpa'at ʃi'nayim	מִרפָּאַת שִינַייִם (נ)
design	itsuv	עִיצוּב (ז)
drugstore, pharmacy	beit mir'kaxat	בֵּית מִרקַחַת (ז)
dry cleaners	nikui yaveʃ	נִיקוּי יָבֵש (ז)
employment agency	soxnut 'koax adam	סוֹכנוּת כּוֹחַ אָדָם (נ)
financial services	ʃerutim fi'nansim	שֵירוּתִים פִינַנסִיים (ז"ר)
food products	mutsrei mazon	מוּצרֵי מָזוֹן (ז"ר)
funeral home	beit levayot	בֵּית לְוָויוֹת (ז)
furniture (e.g., house ~)	rehitim	רָהִיטִים (ז"ר)
clothing, garment	bgadim	בּגָדִים (ז"ר)
hotel	beit malon	בֵּית מָלוֹן (ז)
ice-cream	'glida	גלִידָה (נ)
industry (manufacturing)	ta'asiya	תַעֲשִׂייָה (נ)
insurance	bi'tuax	בִּיטוּחַ (ז)
Internet	'internet	אִינטֶרנֶט (ז)
investments (finance)	haʃka'ot	הַשקָעוֹת (נ"ר)
jeweler	tsoref	צוֹרֵף (ז)
jewelry	taxʃitim	תַכשִיטִים (ז"ר)
laundry (shop)	mixbasa	מִכבָּסָה (נ)
legal advisor	yo'ets miʃpati	יוֹעֵץ מִשפָּטִי (ז)
light industry	ta'asiya kala	תַעֲשִׂייָה קַלָה (נ)
magazine	ʒurnal	ז'וּרנָל (ז)
mail-order selling	mexira be'do'ar	מְכִירָה בְדוֹאַר (נ)
medicine	refu'a	רְפוּאָה (נ)
movie theater	kol'no'a	קוֹלנוֹעַ (ז)
museum	muze'on	מוּזֵיאוֹן (ז)
news agency	soxnut yedi'ot	סוֹכנוּת יְדִיעוֹת (נ)
newspaper	iton	עִיתוֹן (ז)
nightclub	mo'adon 'laila	מוֹעֲדוֹן לַילָה (ז)
oil (petroleum)	neft	נֶפט (ז)
courier services	ʃirut ʃlixim	שֵירוּת שלִיחִים (ז)

pharmaceutics	rokxut	רוֹקְחוּת (נ)
printing (industry)	beit dfus	בֵּית דפוּס (ז)
publishing house	hotsa'a la'or	הוֹצָאָה לָאוֹר (נ)

radio (~ station)	'radyo	רָדִיוֹ (ז)
real estate	nadlan	נַדְלָ"ן (ז)
restaurant	mis'ada	מִסעָדָה (נ)

security company	xevrat ʃmira	חָברַת שמִירָה (נ)
sports	sport	ספּוֹרט (ז)
stock exchange	'bursa	בּוּרסָה (נ)
store	xanut	חָנוּת (נ)
supermarket	super'market	סוּפֶּרמַרקֶט (ז)
swimming pool (public ~)	brexat sxiya	בּרֵיכַת שֹׂחִיָה (נ)

tailor shop	mitpara	מִתפָּרָה (נ)
television	tele'vizya	טֶלֶווִיזיָה (נ)
theater	te'atron	תֵיאַטרוֹן (ז)
trade (commerce)	misxar	מִסֹחָר (ז)
transportation	hovalot	הוֹבָלוֹת (נ״ר)
travel	tayarut	תַיָירוּת (נ)

veterinarian	veterinar	וֶטֶרִינָר (ז)
warehouse	maxsan	מַחסָן (ז)
waste collection	isuf 'zevel	אִיסוּף זֶבֶל (ז)

Job. Business. Part 2

83. Show. Exhibition

exhibition, show	ta'aruxa	תַעֲרוּכָה (נ)
trade show	ta'aruxa misxarit	תַעֲרוּכָה מִסחָרִית (נ)
participation	hiʃtatfut	הִשתַתפוּת (נ)
to participate (vi)	lehiʃtatef	לְהִשתַתֵף
participant (exhibitor)	miʃtatef	מִשתַתֵף (ז)
director	menahel	מְנַהֵל (ז)
organizers' office	misrad hame'argenim	מִשׂרַד הַמְאַרגְנִים (ז)
organizer	me'argen	מְאַרגֵן (ז)
to organize (vt)	le'argen	לְאַרגֵן
participation form	'tofes hiʃtatfut	טוֹפֶס הִשתַתפוּת (ז)
to fill out (vt)	lemale	לְמַלֵא
details	pratim	פּרָטִים (ז"ר)
information	meida	מֵידָע (ז)
price (cost, rate)	mexir	מְחִיר (ז)
including	kolel	כּוֹלֵל
to include (vt)	lixlol	לִכלוֹל
to pay (vi, vt)	leʃalem	לְשַלֵם
registration fee	dmei riʃum	דמֵי רִישוּם (ז"ר)
entrance	knisa	כּנִיסָה (נ)
pavilion, hall	bitan	בִּיתָן (ז)
to register (vt)	lirʃom	לִרשוֹם
badge (identity tag)	tag	תָג (ז)
booth, stand	duxan	דוּכָן (ז)
to reserve, to book	liʃmor	לִשמוֹר
display case	madaf tetsuga	מַדָף תְצוּגָה (ז)
spotlight	menorat spot	מְנוֹרַת ספוֹט (נ)
design	itsuv	עִיצוּב (ז)
to place (put, set)	la'arox	לַעֲרוֹך
to be placed	lehimatse	לְהִימָצֵא
distributor	mefits	מֵפִיץ (ז)
supplier	sapak	סַפָּק (ז)
to supply (vt)	lesapek	לְסַפֵּק
country	medina	מְדִינָה (נ)
foreign (adj)	mexul	מְחוּ"ל

product	mutsar	מוּצָר (ז)
association	amuta	עֲמוּתָה (נ)
conference hall	ulam knasim	אוּלָם כְּנָסִים (ז)
congress	kongres	קוֹנגרֶס (ז)
contest (competition)	taxarut	תַחֲרוּת (נ)
visitor (attendee)	mevaker	מְבַקֵר (ז)
to visit (attend)	levaker	לְבַקֵר
customer	la'koax	לָקוֹחַ (ז)

84. Science. Research. Scientists

science	mada	מַדָע (ז)
scientific (adj)	mada'i	מַדָעִי
scientist	mad'an	מַדעָן (ז)
theory	te''orya	תֵיאוֹריָה (נ)
axiom	aks'yoma	אַקסִיוֹמָה (נ)
analysis	ni'tuax	נִיתוּחַ (ז)
to analyze (vt)	lena'teax	לְנַתֵחַ
argument (strong ~)	nimuk	נִימוּק (ז)
substance (matter)	'xomer	חוֹמֶר (ז)
hypothesis	hipo'teza	הִיפּוֹתֶזָה (נ)
dilemma	di'lema	דִילֶמָה (נ)
dissertation	diser'tatsya	דִיסֶרטַציָה (נ)
dogma	'dogma	דוֹגמָה (נ)
doctrine	dok'trina	דוֹקטרִינָה (נ)
research	mexkar	מֶחקָר (ז)
to research (vt)	laxkor	לַחקוֹר
tests (laboratory ~)	nuisuyim	נִיסוּיִים (ז"ר)
laboratory	ma'abada	מַעֲבָדָה (נ)
method	ʃita	שִיטָה (נ)
molecule	mo'lekula	מוֹלֶקוּלָה (נ)
monitoring	nitur	נִיטוּר (ז)
discovery (act, event)	gilui	גִילוּי (ז)
postulate	aks'yoma	אַקסִיוֹמָה (נ)
principle	ikaron	עִיקָרוֹן (ז)
forecast	taxazit	תַחֲזִית (נ)
to forecast (vt)	laxazot	לַחֲזוֹת
synthesis	sin'teza	סִינתֶזָה (נ)
trend (tendency)	megama	מְגַמָה (נ)
theorem	miʃpat	מִשפָּט (ז)
teachings	tora	תוֹרָה (נ)
fact	uvda	עוּבדָה (נ)

| expedition | miʃˈlaχat | מִשְׁלַחַת (נ) |
| experiment | nisui | נִיסוּי (ז) |

academician	akademai	אָקָדֵמַאי (ז)
bachelor (e.g., ~ of Arts)	'to'ar riʃon	תּוֹאַר רִאשׁוֹן (ז)
doctor (PhD)	'doktor	דּוֹקְטוֹר (ז)
Associate Professor	martse baχir	מַרְצֶה בָּכִיר (ז)
Master (e.g., ~ of Arts)	musmaχ	מוּסְמָךְ (ז)
professor	pro'fesor	פְּרוֹפֶסוֹר (ז)

Professions and occupations

85. Job search. Dismissal

job	avoda	עֲבוֹדָה (נ)
staff (work force)	'segel	סֶגֶל (ז)
personnel	'segel	סֶגֶל (ז)
career	kar'yera	קרִייָרָה (נ)
prospects (chances)	efʃaruyot	אֶפשָׁרוּיוֹת (נ״ר)
skills (mastery)	meyumanut	מְיוּמָנוּת (נ)
selection (screening)	sinun	סִינוּן (ז)
employment agency	soχnut 'koaχ adam	סוֹכנוּת כּוֹחַ אָדָם (נ)
résumé	korot χayim	קוֹרוֹת חַיִים (נ״ר)
job interview	ra'ayon avoda	רַאָיוֹן עֲבוֹדָה (ז)
vacancy, opening	misra pnuya	מִשׂרָה פּנוּיָה (נ)
salary, pay	mas'koret	מַשׂכּוֹרֶת (נ)
fixed salary	mas'koret kvu'a	מַשׂכּוֹרֶת קבוּעָה (נ)
pay, compensation	taʃlum	תַשלוּם (ז)
position (job)	tafkid	תַפקִיד (ז)
duty (of employee)	χova	חוֹבָה (נ)
range of duties	tχum aχrayut	תחוּם אַחרָיוּת (ז)
busy (I'm ~)	asuk	עָסוּק
to fire (dismiss)	lefater	לְפַטֵר
dismissal	pitur	פִּיטוּר (ז)
unemployment	avtala	אַבטָלָה (נ)
unemployed (n)	muvtal	מוּבטָל (ז)
retirement	'pensya	פֶּנסִיָה (נ)
to retire (from job)	laʦet legimla'ot	לָצֵאת לְגִימלָאוֹת

86. Business people

director	menahel	מְנַהֵל (ז)
manager (director)	menahel	מְנַהֵל (ז)
boss	bos	בּוֹס (ז)
superior	memune	מְמוּנֶה (ז)
superiors	memunim	מְמוּנִים (ז״ר)
president	nasi	נָשִׂיא (ז)

chairman	yoʃev roʃ	יוֹשֵׁב רֹאשׁ (ז)
deputy (substitute)	sgan	סְגָן (ז)
assistant	ozer	עוֹזֵר (ז)
secretary	mazkir	מַזְכִּיר (ז)
personal assistant	mazkir iʃi	מַזְכִּיר אִישִׁי (ז)
businessman	iʃ asakim	אִישׁ עֲסָקִים (ז)
entrepreneur	yazam	יָזָם (ז)
founder	meyased	מְיַיסֵד (ז)
to found (vt)	leyased	לְיַיסֵד
incorporator	mexonen	מְכוֹנֵן (ז)
partner	ʃutaf	שׁוּתָף (ז)
stockholder	'ba'al menayot	בַּעַל מְנָיוֹת (ז)
millionaire	milyoner	מִילְיוֹנֶר (ז)
billionaire	milyarder	מִילְיַארְדֶר (ז)
owner, proprietor	be'alim	בְּעָלִים (ז)
landowner	'ba'al adamot	בַּעַל אֲדָמוֹת (ז)
client	la'koax	לָקוֹחַ (ז)
regular client	la'koax ka'vu'a	לָקוֹחַ קָבוּעַ (ז)
buyer (customer)	kone	קוֹנֶה (ז)
visitor	mevaker	מְבַקֵר (ז)
professional (n)	miktso'an	מִקְצוֹעָן (ז)
expert	mumxe	מוּמְחֶה (ז)
specialist	mumxe	מוּמְחֶה (ז)
banker	bankai	בַּנְקַאי (ז)
broker	soxen	סוֹכֵן (ז)
cashier, teller	kupai	קוּפַּאי (ז)
accountant	menahel xeʃbonot	מְנַהֵל חָשְׁבּוֹנוֹת (ז)
security guard	ʃomer	שׁוֹמֵר (ז)
investor	maʃ'ki'a	מַשְׁקִיעַ (ז)
debtor	'ba'al xov	בַּעַל חוֹב (ז)
creditor	malve	מַלְוֶה (ז)
borrower	love	לוֹוֶה (ז)
importer	yevu'an	יְבוּאָן (ז)
exporter	yetsu'an	יְצוּאָן (ז)
manufacturer	yatsran	יַצְרָן (ז)
distributor	mefits	מֵפִיץ (ז)
middleman	metavex	מְתַוֵוךְ (ז)
consultant	yo'ets	יוֹעֵץ (ז)
sales representative	natsig mexirot	נָצִיג מְכִירוֹת (ז)
agent	soxen	סוֹכֵן (ז)
insurance agent	soxen bi'tuax	סוֹכֵן בִּיטוּחַ (ז)

87. Service professions

cook	tabax	טַבָּח (ז)
chef (kitchen chef)	ʃef	שֶׁף (ז)
baker	ofe	אוֹפֶה (ז)
bartender	'barmen	בַּרמֶן (ז)
waiter	meltsar	מֶלצָר (ז)
waitress	meltsarit	מֶלצָרִית (נ)
lawyer, attorney	orex din	עוֹרֵך דִין (ז)
lawyer (legal expert)	orex din	עוֹרֵך דִין (ז)
notary	notaryon	נוֹטַריוֹן (ז)
electrician	xaʃmalai	חַשמְלַאי (ז)
plumber	ʃravrav	שְׁרַבְרָב (ז)
carpenter	nagar	נַגָר (ז)
masseur	maʻase	מְעַסֶה (ז)
masseuse	masa'ʒistit	מַסָז׳יסטִית (נ)
doctor	rofe	רוֹפֵא (ז)
taxi driver	nahag monit	נֶהַג מוֹנִית (ז)
driver	nahag	נֶהַג (ז)
delivery man	ʃa'liax	שָׁלִיחַ (ז)
chambermaid	xadranit	חַדרָנִית (נ)
security guard	ʃomer	שׁוֹמֵר (ז)
flight attendant (fem.)	da'yelet	דַיֶילֶת (נ)
schoolteacher	more	מוֹרָה (ז)
librarian	safran	סַפרָן (ז)
translator	metargem	מְתַרגֵם (ז)
interpreter	meturgeman	מְתוּרגְמָן (ז)
guide	madrix tiyulim	מַדרִיך טִיוּלִים (ז)
hairdresser	sapar	סַפָּר (ז)
mailman	davar	דַוָור (ז)
salesman (store staff)	moxer	מוֹכֵר (ז)
gardener	ganan	גַנָן (ז)
domestic servant	meʃaret	מְשָׁרֵת (ז)
maid (female servant)	meʃa'retet	מְשָׁרַתַת (נ)
cleaner (cleaning lady)	menaka	מְנַקָה (נ)

88. Military professions and ranks

private	turai	טוּרַאי (ז)
sergeant	samal	סַמָל (ז)

lieutenant	'segen	סֶגֶן (ז)
captain	'seren	סֶרֶן (ז)
major	rav 'seren	רַב־סֶרֶן (ז)
colonel	aluf miʃne	אַלוּף מִשְׁנֶה (ז)
general	aluf	אַלוּף (ז)
marshal	'marʃal	מַרְשָׁל (ז)
admiral	admiral	אַדְמִירָל (ז)
military (n)	iʃ tsava	אִישׁ צָבָא (ז)
soldier	χayal	חַיָּל (ז)
officer	katsin	קָצִין (ז)
commander	mefaked	מְפַקֵּד (ז)
border guard	ʃomer gvul	שׁוֹמֵר גְּבוּל (ז)
radio operator	alχutai	אַלְחוּטַאי (ז)
scout (searcher)	iʃ modi'in kravi	אִישׁ מוֹדִיעִין קְרָבִי (ז)
pioneer (sapper)	χablan	חַבְּלָן (ז)
marksman	tsalaf	צַלָּף (ז)
navigator	navat	נַוָּט (ז)

89. Officials. Priests

king	'meleχ	מֶלֶךְ (ז)
queen	malka	מַלְכָּה (נ)
prince	nasiχ	נָסִיךְ (ז)
princess	nesiχa	נְסִיכָה (נ)
czar	tsar	צָאר (ז)
czarina	tsa'rina	צָארִינָה (נ)
president	nasi	נָשִׂיא (ז)
Secretary (minister)	sar	שַׂר (ז)
prime minister	roʃ memʃala	רֹאשׁ מֶמְשָׁלָה (ז)
senator	se'nator	סֶנָאטוֹר (ז)
diplomat	diplomat	דִּיפְּלוֹמָט (ז)
consul	'konsul	קוֹנְסוּל (ז)
ambassador	ʃagrir	שַׁגְרִיר (ז)
counsilor (diplomatic officer)	yo'ets	יוֹעֵץ (ז)
official, functionary (civil servant)	pakid	פָּקִיד (ז)
prefect	prefekt	פְּרֶפֶקְט (ז)
mayor	roʃ ha'ir	רֹאשׁ הָעִיר (ז)
judge	ʃofet	שׁוֹפֵט (ז)
prosecutor (e.g., district attorney)	to've'a	תּוֹבֵעַ (ז)

missionary	misyoner	מִיסיוֹנֶר (ז)
monk	nazir	נָזִיר (ז)
abbot	roʃ minzar ka'toli	ראש מִנזָר קָתוֹלִי (ז)
rabbi	rav	רַב (ז)
vizier	vazir	וָזִיר (ז)
shah	ʃax	שָׁאח (ז)
sheikh	ʃeix	שֵׁיח (ז)

90. Agricultural professions

beekeeper	kavran	כַּווָרָן (ז)
herder, shepherd	ro'e tson	רוֹעֵה צֹאן (ז)
agronomist	agronom	אַגרוֹנוֹם (ז)
cattle breeder	megadel bakar	מְגַדֵל בָּקָר (ז)
veterinarian	veterinar	וֶטֶרִינָר (ז)
farmer	xavai	חַווַאי (ז)
winemaker	yeinan	יֵינָן (ז)
zoologist	zo'olog	זוֹאוֹלוֹג (ז)
cowboy	'ka'uboi	קָאוּבּוֹי (ז)

91. Art professions

actor	saxkan	שַׂחקָן (ז)
actress	saxkanit	שַׂחקָנִית (נ)
singer (masc.)	zamar	זַמָר (ז)
singer (fem.)	za'meret	זַמֶרֶת (נ)
dancer (masc.)	rakdan	רַקדָן (ז)
dancer (fem.)	rakdanit	רַקדָנִית (נ)
performer (masc.)	saxkan	שַׂחקָן (ז)
performer (fem.)	saxkanit	שַׂחקָנִית (נ)
musician	muzikai	מוּזִיקָאי (ז)
pianist	psantran	פְּסַנתְרָן (ז)
guitar player	nagan gi'tara	נַגָן גִיטָרָה (ז)
conductor (orchestra ~)	mena'tseax	מְנַצֵחַ (ז)
composer	malxin	מַלחִין (ז)
impresario	amargan	אָמַרגָן (ז)
film director	bamai	בַּמַאי (ז)
producer	mefik	מֵפִיק (ז)
scriptwriter	tasritai	תַסרִיטַאי (ז)
critic	mevaker	מְבַקֵר (ז)

writer	sofer	סוֹפֵר (ז)
poet	meʃorer	מְשׁוֹרֵר (ז)
sculptor	pasal	פַּסָל (ז)
artist (painter)	tsayar	צַיָיר (ז)

juggler	lahatutan	לַהֲטוּטָן (ז)
clown	leitsan	לֵיצָן (ז)
acrobat	akrobat	אַקרוֹבָּט (ז)
magician	kosem	קוֹסֵם (ז)

92. Various professions

doctor	rofe	רוֹפֵא (ז)
nurse	aχot	אָחוֹת (נ)
psychiatrist	psiχi''ater	פּסִיכִיאָטֶר (ז)
dentist	rofe ʃi'nayim	רוֹפֵא שִינַיִים (ז)
surgeon	kirurg	כִּירוּרג (ז)

astronaut	astro'na'ut	אַסטרוֹנָאוּט (ז)
astronomer	astronom	אַסטרוֹנוֹם (ז)
pilot	tayas	טַיָיס (ז)

driver (of taxi, etc.)	nahag	נַהָג (ז)
engineer (train driver)	nahag ra'kevet	נַהָג רַכֶּבֶת (ז)
mechanic	meχonai	מְכוֹנַאי (ז)

miner	kore	כּוֹרֶה (ז)
worker	po'el	פּוֹעֵל (ז)
locksmith	misgad	מִסגָד (ז)
joiner (carpenter)	nagar	נַגָר (ז)
turner (lathe machine operator)	χarat	חָרָט (ז)
construction worker	banai	בַּנַאי (ז)
welder	rataχ	רַתָך (ז)

professor (title)	pro'fesor	פּרוֹפֶסוֹר (ז)
architect	adriχal	אַדרִיכָל (ז)
historian	historyon	הִיסטוֹריוֹן (ז)
scientist	mad'an	מַדעָן (ז)
physicist	fizikai	פִיזִיקָאי (ז)
chemist (scientist)	χimai	כִימָאי (ז)

archeologist	arχe'olog	אַרכֵיאוֹלוֹג (ז)
geologist	ge'olog	גֵיאוֹלוֹג (ז)
researcher (scientist)	χoker	חוֹקֵר (ז)

babysitter	ʃmartaf	שמַרטָף (ז)
teacher, educator	more, meχaneχ	מוֹרֶה, מְחַנֵך (ז)
editor	oreχ	עוֹרֵך (ז)
editor-in-chief	oreχ raʃi	עוֹרֵך רָאשִי (ז)

correspondent	katav	כַּתָב (ז)
typist (fem.)	kaldanit	קַלְדָנִית (נ)
designer	me'atsev	מְעַצֵב (ז)
computer expert	mumxe maxʃevim	מוּמחֶה מַחשְבִים (ז)
programmer	metaxnet	מְתַכנֵת (ז)
engineer (designer)	mehandes	מְהַנדֵס (ז)
sailor	yamai	יַמַאי (ז)
seaman	malax	מַלָח (ז)
rescuer	matsil	מַצִיל (ז)
fireman	kabai	כַּבַּאי (ז)
police officer	ʃoter	שוֹטֵר (ז)
watchman	ʃomer	שוֹמֵר (ז)
detective	balaʃ	בַּלָש (ז)
customs officer	pakid 'mexes	פָּקִיד מֶכֶס (ז)
bodyguard	ʃomer roʃ	שוֹמֵר ראש (ז)
prison guard	soher	סוֹהֵר (ז)
inspector	mefa'keax	מְפַקֵח (ז)
sportsman	sportai	ספּוֹרטַאי (ז)
trainer, coach	me'amen	מְאַמֵן (ז)
butcher	katsav	קַצָב (ז)
cobbler (shoe repairer)	sandlar	סַנדלָר (ז)
merchant	soxer	סוֹחֵר (ז)
loader (person)	sabal	סַבָּל (ז)
fashion designer	me'atsev ofna	מְעַצֵב אוֹפנָה (ז)
model (fem.)	dugmanit	דוּגמָנִית (נ)

93. Occupations. Social status

schoolboy	talmid	תַלמִיד (ז)
student (college ~)	student	סטוּדֶנט (ז)
philosopher	filosof	פִילוֹסוֹף (ז)
economist	kalkelan	כַּלכְּלָן (ז)
inventor	mamtsi	מַמצִיא (ז)
unemployed (n)	muvtal	מוּבטָל (ז)
retiree	pensyoner	פֶּנסיוֹנֵר (ז)
spy, secret agent	meragel	מְרַגֵל (ז)
prisoner	asir	אָסִיר (ז)
striker	ʃovet	שוֹבֵת (ז)
bureaucrat	birokrat	בִּירוֹקרָט (ז)
traveler (globetrotter)	metayel	מְטַיֵיל (ז)
gay, homosexual (n)	'lesbit, 'homo	לֶסבִּית (נ), הוֹמוֹ (ז)

hacker	'haker	הָאקֶר (ז)
hippie	'hipi	הִיפִּי (ז)
bandit	ʃoded	שׁוֹדֵד (ז)
hit man, killer	ro'tseaχ saχir	רוֹצֵחַ שָׂכִיר (ז)
drug addict	narkoman	נַרקוֹמָן (ז)
drug dealer	soχer samim	סוֹחֵר סַמִּים (ז)
prostitute (fem.)	zona	זוֹנָה (נ)
pimp	sarsur	סַרסוּר (ז)
sorcerer	meχaʃef	מְכַשֵּׁף (ז)
sorceress (evil ~)	maχʃefa	מַכשֵׁפָה (נ)
pirate	ʃoded yam	שׁוֹדֵד יָם (ז)
slave	ʃifχa, 'eved	שִׁפחָה (נ), עֶבֶד (ז)
samurai	samurai	סָמוּרַאי (ז)
savage (primitive)	'pere adam	פֶּרֶא אָדָם (ז)

Education

94. School

school	beit 'sefer	בֵּית סֵפֶר (ז)
principal (headmaster)	menahel beit 'sefer	מְנַהֵל בֵּית סֵפֶר (ז)
pupil (boy)	talmid	תַלְמִיד (ז)
pupil (girl)	talmida	תַלְמִידָה (נ)
schoolboy	talmid	תַלְמִיד (ז)
schoolgirl	talmida	תַלְמִידָה (נ)
to teach (sb)	lelamed	לְלַמֵד
to learn (language, etc.)	lilmod	לִלְמוֹד
to learn by heart	lilmod be'al pe	לִלְמוֹד בְּעַל פֶּה
to learn (~ to count, etc.)	lilmod	לִלְמוֹד
to be in school	lilmod	לִלְמוֹד
to go to school	la'leχet le'beit 'sefer	לָלֶכֶת לְבֵית סֵפֶר
alphabet	alefbeit	אָלֶפבֵּית (ז)
subject (at school)	mik'tso'a	מִקְצוֹעַ (ז)
classroom	kita	כִּיתָה (נ)
lesson	ʃi'ur	שִיעוּר (ז)
recess	hafsaka	הַפסָקָה (נ)
school bell	pa'amon	פַּעֲמוֹן (ז)
school desk	ʃulχan limudim	שוּלחַן לִימוּדִים (ז)
chalkboard	'luaχ	לוּחַ (ז)
grade	tsiyun	צִיוּן (ז)
good grade	tsiyun tov	צִיוּן טוֹב (ז)
bad grade	tsiyun ga'ru'a	צִיוּן גָרוּעַ (ז)
to give a grade	latet tsiyun	לָתֵת צִיוּן
mistake, error	ta'ut	טָעוּת (נ)
to make mistakes	la'asot ta'uyot	לַעֲשׂוֹת טָעוּיוֹת
to correct (an error)	letaken	לְתַקֵן
cheat sheet	ʃlif	שלִיף (ז)
homework	ʃi'urei 'bayit	שִיעוּרֵי בַּיִת (ז״ר)
exercise (in education)	targil	תַרגִיל (ז)
to be present	lihyot no'χeaχ	לִהיוֹת נוֹכֵחַ
to be absent	lehe'ader	לְהֵיעָדֵר
to miss school	lehaχsir	לְהַחסִיר

to punish (vt)	leha'aniʃ	לְהַעֲנִישׁ
punishment	'oneʃ	עוֹנֶשׁ (ז)
conduct (behavior)	hitnahagut	הִתְנַהֲגוּת (נ)
report card	yoman beit 'sefer	יוֹמָן בֵּית סָפֶר (ז)
pencil	iparon	עִיפָּרוֹן (ז)
eraser	'maxak	מַחַק (ז)
chalk	gir	גִיר (ז)
pencil case	kalmar	קַלמָר (ז)
schoolbag	yalkut	יַלקוּט (ז)
pen	et	עֵט (ז)
school notebook	max'beret	מַחבֶּרֶת (נ)
textbook	'sefer limud	סָפֶר לִימוּד (ז)
compasses	mexuga	מְחוּגָה (נ)
to make technical drawings	lesartet	לְשַׂרטֵט
technical drawing	sirtut	שִׂרטוּט (ז)
poem	ʃir	שִׁיר (ז)
by heart (adv)	be'al pe	בְּעַל פֶּה
to learn by heart	lilmod be'al pe	לִלמוֹד בְּעַל פֶּה
school vacation	xufʃa	חוּפשָׁה (נ)
to be on vacation	lihyot bexufʃa	לִהיוֹת בְּחוּפשָׁה
to spend one's vacation	leha'avir 'xofeʃ	לְהַעֲבִיר חוֹפֶשׁ
test (written math ~)	mivxan	מִבחָן (ז)
essay (composition)	xibur	חִיבּוּר (ז)
dictation	haxtava	הַכתָבָה (נ)
exam (examination)	bxina	בּחִינָה (נ)
to take an exam	lehibaxen	לְהִיבָּחֵן
experiment (e.g., chemistry ~)	nisui	נִיסוּי (ז)

95. College. University

academy	aka'demya	אָקָדֶמיָה (נ)
university	uni'versita	אוּנִיבֶרסִיטָה (נ)
faculty (e.g., ~ of Medicine)	fa'kulta	פָקוּלטָה (נ)
student (masc.)	student	סטוּדֶנט (ז)
student (fem.)	stu'dentit	סטוּדֶנטִית (נ)
lecturer (teacher)	martse	מַרצֶה (ז)
lecture hall, room	ulam hartsa'ot	אוּלַם הַרצָאוֹת (ז)
graduate	boger	בּוֹגֵר (ז)
diploma	di'ploma	דִיפלוֹמָה (נ)

dissertation	diser'tatsya	דִיסֶרְטַצְיָה (נ)
study (report)	meχkar	מֶחְקָר (ז)
laboratory	ma'abada	מַעֲבָּדָה (נ)
lecture	hartsa'a	הַרְצָאָה (נ)
coursemate	χaver lelimudim	חָבֵר לְלִימוּדִים (ז)
scholarship	milga	מִלְגָה (נ)
academic degree	'to'ar aka'demi	תוֹאַר אָקָדֶמִי (ז)

96. Sciences. Disciplines

mathematics	mate'matika	מָתֶמָטִיקָה (נ)
algebra	'algebra	אַלְגֶבְּרָה (נ)
geometry	ge'o'metriya	גֵיאוֹמֶטְרִיָה (נ)
astronomy	astro'nomya	אַסטרוֹנוֹמִיָה (נ)
biology	bio'logya	בִּיוֹלוֹגְיָה (נ)
geography	ge'o'grafya	גֵיאוֹגְרַפְיָה (נ)
geology	ge'o'logya	גֵיאוֹלוֹגְיָה (נ)
history	his'torya	הִיסטוֹרִיָה (נ)
medicine	refu'a	רְפוּאָה (נ)
pedagogy	χinuχ	חִינוּךְ (ז)
law	miʃpatim	מִשׁפָּטִים (ז"ר)
physics	'fizika	פִיזִיקָה (נ)
chemistry	'χimya	כִימִיָה (נ)
philosophy	filo'sofya	פִילוֹסוֹפְיָה (נ)
psychology	psiχo'logya	פסִיכוֹלוֹגְיָה (נ)

97. Writing system. Orthography

grammar	dikduk	דִקדוּק (ז)
vocabulary	otsar milim	אוֹצָר מִילִים (ז)
phonetics	torat ha'hege	תוֹרַת הַהֲגָה (נ)
noun	ʃem 'etsem	שֵׁם עָצָם (ז)
adjective	ʃem 'to'ar	שֵׁם תוֹאַר (ז)
verb	po'el	פוֹעַל (ז)
adverb	'to'ar 'po'al	תוֹאַר פוֹעַל (ז)
pronoun	ʃem guf	שֵׁם גוּף (ז)
interjection	milat kri'a	מִילַת קרִיאָה (נ)
preposition	milat 'yaχas	מִילַת יַחַס (נ)
root	'ʃoreʃ	שוֹרֶשׁ (ז)
ending	si'yomet	סִיוֹמֶת (נ)
prefix	tχilit	תחִילִית (נ)

syllable	havara	הֲבָרָה (נ)
suffix	si'yomet	סִיוֹמֶת (נ)
stress mark	'ta'am	טַעַם (ז)
apostrophe	'gereʃ	גֶרֶשׁ (ז)
period, dot	nekuda	נְקוּדָה (נ)
comma	psik	פְּסִיק (ז)
semicolon	nekuda ufsik	נְקוּדָה וּפְסִיק (נ)
colon	nekudo'tayim	נְקוּדוֹתַיִים (נ"ר)
ellipsis	ʃaloʃ nekudot	שָׁלוֹשׁ נְקוּדוֹת (נ"ר)
question mark	siman ʃe'ela	סִימָן שְׁאֵלָה (ז)
exclamation point	siman kri'a	סִימָן קְרִיאָה (ז)
quotation marks	merχa'ot	מֵרְכָאוֹת (נ"ר)
in quotation marks	bemerχa'ot	בְּמֵרְכָאוֹת
parenthesis	sog'rayim	סוֹגְרַיִים (ז"ר)
in parenthesis	besog'rayim	בְּסוֹגְרַיִים
hyphen	makaf	מַקָף (ז)
dash	kav mafrid	קַו מַפְרִיד (ז)
space (between words)	'revaχ	רֶוַח (ז)
letter	ot	אוֹת (נ)
capital letter	ot gdola	אוֹת גְדוֹלָה (נ)
vowel (n)	tnu'a	תְנוּעָה (נ)
consonant (n)	itsur	עִיצוּר (ז)
sentence	miʃpat	מִשְׁפָּט (ז)
subject	nose	נוֹשֵׂא (ז)
predicate	nasu	נָשׂוּא (ז)
line	ʃura	שׁוּרָה (נ)
on a new line	beʃura χadaʃa	בְּשׁוּרָה חֲדָשָׁה
paragraph	piska	פְּסְקָה (נ)
word	mila	מִילָה (נ)
group of words	tsiruf milim	צֵירוּף מִילִים (ז)
expression	bitui	בִּיטוּי (ז)
synonym	mila nir'defet	מִילָה נִרְדֶפֶת (נ)
antonym	'hefeχ	הֶפֶךְ (ז)
rule	klal	כְּלָל (ז)
exception	yotse min haklal	יוֹצֵא מִן הַכְּלָל (ז)
correct (adj)	naχon	נָכוֹן
conjugation	hataya	הַטָיָיה (נ)
declension	hataya	הַטָיָיה (נ)
nominal case	yaχasa	יַחֲסָה (נ)
question	ʃe'ela	שְׁאֵלָה (נ)

to underline (vt)	lehadgiʃ	לְהַדְגִּישׁ
dotted line	kav nakud	קַו נָקוּד (ז)

98. Foreign languages

language	safa	שָׂפָה (נ)
foreign (adj)	zar	זָר
foreign language	safa zara	שָׂפָה זָרָה (נ)
to study (vt)	lilmod	לִלְמוֹד
to learn (language, etc.)	lilmod	לִלְמוֹד
to read (vi, vt)	likro	לִקְרוֹא
to speak (vi, vt)	ledaber	לְדַבֵּר
to understand (vt)	lehavin	לְהָבִין
to write (vt)	lixtov	לִכְתּוֹב
fast (adv)	maher	מַהֵר
slowly (adv)	le'at	לְאַט
fluently (adv)	xofʃi	חוֹפְשִׁי
rules	klalim	כְּלָלִים (ז״ר)
grammar	dikduk	דִּקְדּוּק (ז)
vocabulary	otsar milim	אוֹצַר מִילִים (ז)
phonetics	torat ha'hege	תּוֹרַת הַהֲגָה (נ)
textbook	'sefer limud	סֵפֶר לִימוּד (ז)
dictionary	milon	מִילוֹן (ז)
teach-yourself book	'sefer lelimud atsmi	סֵפֶר לְלִימוּד עַצְמִי (ז)
phrasebook	sixon	שִׂיחוֹן (ז)
cassette, tape	ka'letet	קַלֶּטֶת (נ)
videotape	ka'letet 'vide'o	קַלֶּטֶת וִידִיאוֹ (נ)
CD, compact disc	taklitor	תַּקְלִיטוֹר (ז)
DVD	di vi di	דִי. וִי. דִי. (ז)
alphabet	alefbeit	אָלֶפְבֵּית (ז)
to spell (vt)	le'ayet	לְאַיֵּית
pronunciation	hagiya	הֲגִיָּיה (נ)
accent	mivta	מִבְטָא (ז)
with an accent	im mivta	עִם מִבְטָא
without an accent	bli mivta	בְּלִי מִבְטָא
word	mila	מִילָה (נ)
meaning	maʃma'ut	מַשְׁמָעוּת (נ)
course (e.g., a French ~)	kurs	קוּרְס (ז)
to sign up	leheraʃem lekurs	לְהֵירָשֵׁם לְקוּרְס
teacher	more	מוֹרֶה (ז)
translation (process)	tirgum	תַּרְגּוּם (ז)

translation (text, etc.)	tirgum	תִרְגוּם (ז)
translator	metargem	מְתַרְגֵם (ז)
interpreter	meturgeman	מְתוּרְגְמָן (ז)
polyglot	poliglot	פּוֹליגלוֹט (ז)
memory	zikaron	זִיכָּרוֹן (ז)

Rest. Entertainment. Travel

99. Trip. Travel

tourism, travel	tayarut	תַּיָירוּת (נ)
tourist	tayar	תַּיָיר (ז)
trip, voyage	tiyul	טִיוּל (ז)
adventure	harpatka	הַרפַּתקָה (נ)
trip, journey	nesi'a	נְסִיעָה (נ)
vacation	ḥuffa	חוּפשָה (נ)
to be on vacation	lihyot beḥuffa	לִהיוֹת בְּחוּפשָה
rest	menuḥa	מְנוּחָה (נ)
train	ra'kevet	רַכֶּבֶת (נ)
by train	bera'kevet	בְּרַכֶּבֶת
airplane	matos	מָטוֹס (ז)
by airplane	bematos	בְּמָטוֹס
by car	bemeḥonit	בִּמכוֹנִית
by ship	be'oniya	בְּאוֹנִייָה
luggage	mit'an	מִטעָן (ז)
suitcase	mizvada	מִזווָדָה (נ)
luggage cart	eglat mit'an	עֶגלַת מִטעָן (נ)
passport	darkon	דַרכּוֹן (ז)
visa	'viza, aſra	וִיזָה, אַשׁרָה (נ)
ticket	kartis	כַּרטִיס (ז)
air ticket	kartis tisa	כַּרטִיס טִיסָה (ז)
guidebook	madriḥ	מַדרִיך (ז)
map (tourist ~)	mapa	מַפָּה (נ)
area (rural ~)	ezor	אָזוֹר (ז)
place, site	makom	מָקוֹם (ז)
exotica (n)	ek'zotika	אֶקזוֹטִיקָה (נ)
exotic (adj)	ek'zoti	אֶקזוֹטִי
amazing (adj)	nifla	נִפלָא
group	kvutsa	קבוּצָה (נ)
excursion, sightseeing tour	tiyul	טִיוּל (ז)
guide (person)	madriḥ tiyulim	מַדרִיך טִיוּלִים (ז)

100. Hotel

hotel	malon	מָלוֹן (ז)
motel	motel	מוֹטֵל (ז)
three-star (~ hotel)	ʃloʃa koxavim	שְׁלוֹשָׁה כּוֹכָבִים
five-star	xamiʃa koxavim	חֲמִישָׁה כּוֹכָבִים
to stay (in a hotel, etc.)	lehit'axsen	לְהִתְאַכְסֵן
room	'xeder	חֶדֶר (ז)
single room	'xeder yaxid	חֶדֶר יָחִיד (ז)
double room	'xeder zugi	חֶדֶר זוּגִי (ז)
to book a room	lehazmin 'xeder	לְהַזמִין חֶדֶר
half board	xatsi pensiyon	חֲצִי פֶּנסִיוֹן (ז)
full board	pensyon male	פֶּנסִיוֹן מָלֵא (ז)
with bath	im am'batya	עִם אַמבַּטיָה
with shower	im mik'laxat	עִם מִקלַחַת
satellite television	tele'vizya bekvalim	טֶלֶוִוִיזיָה בְּכבָלִים (נ)
air-conditioner	mazgan	מַזגָן (ז)
towel	ma'gevet	מַגֶבֶת (נ)
key	maf'teax	מַפתֵחַ (ז)
administrator	amarkal	אֲמַרכָּל (ז)
chambermaid	xadranit	חַדרָנִית (נ)
porter, bellboy	sabal	סַבָּל (ז)
doorman	pakid kabala	פְּקִיד קַבָּלָה (ז)
restaurant	mis'ada	מִסעָדָה (נ)
pub, bar	bar	בָּר (ז)
breakfast	aruxat 'boker	אֲרוּחַת בּוֹקֶר (נ)
dinner	aruxat 'erev	אֲרוּחַת עֶרֶב (נ)
buffet	miznon	מִזנוֹן (ז)
lobby	'lobi	לוֹבִּי (ז)
elevator	ma'alit	מַעֲלִית (נ)
DO NOT DISTURB	lo lehaf'ri'a	לֹא לְהַפרִיעַ
NO SMOKING	asur le'aʃen!	אָסוּר לְעַשֵׁן!

TECHNICAL EQUIPMENT. TRANSPORTATION

Technical equipment

101. Computer

computer	maxʃev	מַחשֵׁב (ז)
notebook, laptop	maxʃev nayad	מַחשֵׁב נַייָד (ז)
to turn on	lehadlik	לְהַדלִיק
to turn off	lexabot	לְכַבּוֹת
keyboard	mik'ledet	מִקלֶדֶת (נ)
key	makaʃ	מַקָש (ז)
mouse	axbar	עַכבָּר (ז)
mouse pad	ʃa'tiax le'axbar	שָׁטִיחַ לְעַכבָּר (ז)
button	kaftor	כַּפתוֹר (ז)
cursor	saman	סַמָן (ז)
monitor	masax	מָסָך (ז)
screen	tsag	צַג (ז)
hard disk	disk ka'ʃiax	דִיסק קָשִׁיחַ (ז)
hard disk capacity	'nefax disk ka'ʃiax	נֶפַח דִיסק קָשִׁיחַ (ז)
memory	zikaron	זִיכָּרוֹן (ז)
random access memory	zikaron giʃa akra'it	זִיכָּרוֹן גִישָׁה אַקרָאִית (ז)
file	'kovets	קוֹבֶץ (ז)
folder	tikiya	תִיקִייָה (נ)
to open (vt)	lif'toax	לִפתוֹחַ
to close (vt)	lisgor	לִסגוֹר
to save (vt)	liʃmor	לִשמוֹר
to delete (vt)	limxok	לִמחוֹק
to copy (vt)	leha'atik	לְהַעֲתִיק
to sort (vt)	lemayen	לְמַיֵן
to transfer (copy)	leha'avir	לְהַעֲבִיר
program	toxna	תוֹכנָה (נ)
software	toxna	תוֹכנָה (נ)
programmer	metaxnet	מְתַכנֵת (ז)
to program (vt)	letaxnet	לְתַכנֵת
hacker	'haker	הָאקֶר (ז)
password	sisma	סִיסמָה (נ)

virus	'virus	וִירוּס (ז)
to find, to detect	limtso, le'ater	לִמְצוֹא, לְאַתֵּר
byte	bait	בַּייט (ז)
megabyte	megabait	מֶגָבַּייט (ז)
data	netunim	נְתוּנִים (ז"ר)
database	bsis netunim	בְּסִיס נְתוּנִים (ז)
cable (USB, etc.)	'kevel	כֶּבֶל (ז)
to disconnect (vt)	lenatek	לְנַתֵּק
to connect (sth to sth)	leχaber	לְחַבֵּר

102. Internet. E-mail

Internet	'internet	אִינטֶרנֶט (ז)
browser	dafdefan	דַפדְפָן (ז)
search engine	ma'no'a χipus	מָנוֹעַ חִיפּוּשׂ (ז)
provider	sapak	סַפָּק (ז)
webmaster	menahel ha'atar	מְנַהֵל הָאָתָר (ז)
website	atar	אָתָר (ז)
webpage	daf 'internet	דַף אִינטֶרנֶט (ז)
address (e-mail ~)	'ktovet	כּתוֹבֶת (נ)
address book	'sefer ktovot	סֵפֶר כּתוֹבוֹת (ז)
mailbox	teivat 'do'ar	תֵיבַת דוֹאַר (נ)
mail	'do'ar, 'do'al	דוֹאַר (ז), דוֹא"ל (ז)
full (adj)	gaduʃ	גָדוּשׁ
message	hoda'a	הוֹדָעָה (נ)
incoming messages	hoda'ot niχnasot	הוֹדָעוֹת נִכנָסוֹת (נ"ר)
outgoing messages	hoda'ot yots'ot	הוֹדָעוֹת יוֹצאוֹת (נ"ר)
sender	ʃo'leaχ	שׁוֹלֵחַ (ז)
to send (vt)	liʃ'loaχ	לִשׁלוֹחַ
sending (of mail)	ʃliχa	שׁלִיחָה (נ)
receiver	nim'an	נִמעָן (ז)
to receive (vt)	lekabel	לְקַבֵּל
correspondence	hitkatvut	הִתכַּתבוּת (נ)
to correspond (vi)	lehitkatev	לְהִתכַּתֵב
file	'kovets	קוֹבֶץ (ז)
to download (vt)	lehorid	לְהוֹרִיד
to create (vt)	litsor	לִיצוֹר
to delete (vt)	limχok	לִמחוֹק
deleted (adj)	maχuk	מָחוּק
connection (ADSL, etc.)	χibur	חִיבּוּר (ז)

speed	mehirut	מְהִירוּת (נ)
modem	'modem	מוֹדֶם (ז)
access	giʃa	גִישָׁה (נ)
port (e.g., input ~)	port	פּוֹרט (ז)
connection (make a ~)	xibur	חִיבּוּר (ז)
to connect to ... (vi)	lehitxaber	לְהִתחַבֵּר
to select (vt)	livxor	לִבחוֹר
to search (for ...)	lexapes	לְחַפֵּשׂ

103. Electricity

electricity	xaʃmal	חַשמַל (ז)
electric, electrical (adj)	xaʃmali	חַשמַלִי
electric power plant	taxanat 'koax	תַחֲנַת כּוֹחַ (נ)
energy	e'nergya	אֶנֶרגיָה (נ)
electric power	e'nergya xaʃmalit	אֶנֶרגיָה חַשמַלִית (נ)
light bulb	nura	נוּרָה (נ)
flashlight	panas	פָּנָס (ז)
street light	panas rexov	פָּנָס רְחוֹב (ז)
light	or	אוֹר (ז)
to turn on	lehadlik	לְהַדלִיק
to turn off	lexabot	לְכַבּוֹת
to turn off the light	lexabot	לְכַבּוֹת
to burn out (vi)	lehisaref	לְהִישָׂרֵף
short circuit	'ketser	קֶצֶר (ז)
broken wire	xut ka'ru'a	חוּט קָרוּעַ (ז)
contact (electrical ~)	maga	מַגָע (ז)
light switch	'meteg	מֶתֶג (ז)
wall socket	'ʃeka	שֶׁקַע (ז)
plug	'teka	תֶקַע (ז)
extension cord	'kabel ma'arix	כַּבֶל מַאֲרִיך (ז)
fuse	natix	נָתִיך (ז)
cable, wire	xut	חוּט (ז)
wiring	xivut	חִיווּט (ז)
ampere	amper	אַמפֵּר (ז)
amperage	'zerem xaʃmali	זֶרֶם חַשמַלִי (ז)
volt	volt	ווֹלט (ז)
voltage	'metax	מֶתַח (ז)
electrical device	maxʃir xaʃmali	מַכשִׁיר חַשמַלִי (ז)
indicator	maxvan	מַחווָן (ז)
electrician	xaʃmalai	חַשמַלַאי (ז)

to solder (vt)	lehalxim	לְהַלְחִים
soldering iron	malxem	מַלְחֵם (ז)
electric current	'zerem	זֶרֶם (ז)

104. Tools

tool, instrument	kli	כְּלִי (ז)
tools	klei avoda	כְּלֵי עֲבוֹדָה (ז"ר)
equipment (factory ~)	tsiyud	צִיוּד (ז)
hammer	patiʃ	פַּטִיש (ז)
screwdriver	mavreg	מַברֵג (ז)
ax	garzen	גַרזֶן (ז)
saw	masor	מַסוֹר (ז)
to saw (vt)	lenaser	לְנַסֵר
plane (tool)	maktso'a	מַקצוּעָה (נ)
to plane (vt)	lehak'tsi'a	לְהַקצִיעַ
soldering iron	malxem	מַלחֵם (ז)
to solder (vt)	lehalxim	לְהַלחִים
file (tool)	ptsira	פּצִירָה (נ)
carpenter pincers	tsvatot	צבָתוֹת (ני"ר)
lineman's pliers	mel'kaxat	מֶלקַחַת (נ)
chisel	izmel	אָזמֵל (ז)
drill bit	mak'deax	מַקדֵחַ (ז)
electric drill	makdexa	מַקדֵחָה (נ)
to drill (vi, vt)	lik'doax	לִקדוֹחַ
knife	sakin	סַכִּין (ז, נ)
pocket knife	olar	אוֹלָר (ז)
blade	'lahav	לַהַב (ז)
sharp (blade, etc.)	xad	חַד
dull, blunt (adj)	kehe	קֵהֶה
to get blunt (dull)	lehitkahot	לְהִתקַהוֹת
to sharpen (vt)	lehaʃxiz	לְהַשחִיז
bolt	'boreg	בּוֹרֶג (ז)
nut	om	אוֹם (ז)
thread (of a screw)	tavrig	תַברִיג (ז)
wood screw	'boreg	בּוֹרֶג (ז)
nail	masmer	מַסמֵר (ז)
nailhead	roʃ hamasmer	רֹאש הַמַסמֵר (ז)
ruler (for measuring)	sargel	סַרגֵל (ז)
tape measure	'seret meida	סֶרֶט מֵידָה (ז)
spirit level	'peles	פֶּלֶס (ז)

magnifying glass	zxuxit mag'delet	זְכוּכִית מַגְדֶלֶת (נ)
measuring instrument	maxʃir medida	מַכְשִׁיר מְדִידָה (ז)
to measure (vt)	limdod	לִמְדוֹד
scale (of thermometer, etc.)	'skala	סְקָאלָה (נ)
readings	medida	מְדִידָה (נ)
compressor	madxes	מַדְחֵס (ז)
microscope	mikroskop	מִיקְרוֹסקוֹפּ (ז)
pump (e.g., water ~)	maʃeva	מַשְׁאֵבָה (נ)
robot	robot	רוֹבּוֹט (ז)
laser	'leizer	לַייזֶר (ז)
wrench	maf'teax bragim	מַפְתֵחַ בְּרָגִים (ז)
adhesive tape	neyar 'devek	נְייַר דֶבֶק (ז)
glue	'devek	דֶבֶק (ז)
sandpaper	neyar zxuxit	נְייַר זְכוּכִית (ז)
spring	kfits	קְפִיץ (ז)
magnet	magnet	מַגנֶט (ז)
gloves	kfafot	כְּפָפוֹת (נ״ר)
rope	'xevel	חֶבֶל (ז)
cord	srox	שְׂרוֹך (ז)
wire (e.g., telephone ~)	xut	חוּט (ז)
cable	'kevel	כֶּבֶל (ז)
sledgehammer	kurnas	קוּרנָס (ז)
prybar	lom	לוֹם (ז)
ladder	sulam	סוּלָם (ז)
stepladder	sulam	סוּלָם (ז)
to screw (tighten)	lehavrig	לְהַבְרִיג
to unscrew (lid, filter, etc.)	lif'toax, lehavrig	לִפְתוֹחַ, לְהַבְרִיג
to tighten (e.g., with a clamp)	lehadek	לְהַדֵק
to glue, to stick	lehadbik	לְהַדְבִּיק
to cut (vt)	laxtox	לַחְתוֹך
malfunction (fault)	takala	תַקָלָה (נ)
repair (mending)	tikun	תִיקוּן (ז)
to repair, to fix (vt)	letaken	לְתַקֵן
to adjust (machine, etc.)	lexavnen	לְכַווֵנֵן
to check (to examine)	livdok	לִבדוֹק
checking	bdika	בְּדִיקָה (נ)
readings	kri'a	קְרִיאָה (נ)
reliable, solid (machine)	amin	אָמִין
complex (adj)	murkav	מוּרכָּב
to rust (get rusted)	lehaxlid	לְהַחֲלִיד

| rusty, rusted (adj) | χalud | חָלוּד |
| rust | χaluda | חֲלוּדָה (נ) |

Transportation

105. Airplane

airplane	matos	מָטוֹס (ז)
air ticket	kartis tisa	כַּרטִיס טִיסָה (ז)
airline	xevrat te'ufa	חֶברַת תְעוּפָה (נ)
airport	nemal te'ufa	נְמַל תְעוּפָה (ז)
supersonic (adj)	al koli	עַל קוֹלִי
captain	kabarnit	קַבַּרנִיט (ז)
crew	'tsevet	צֶוֶת (ז)
pilot	tayas	טַיָיס (ז)
flight attendant (fem.)	da'yelet	דַיֶילֶת (נ)
navigator	navat	נַוָוט (ז)
wings	kna'fayim	כְּנָפַיִים (נ״ר)
tail	zanav	זָנָב (ז)
cockpit	'kokpit	קוֹקפִּיט (ז)
engine	ma'no'a	מָנוֹעַ (ז)
undercarriage (landing gear)	kan nesi'a	כַּן נְסִיעָה (ז)
turbine	tur'bina	טורבִּינָה (נ)
propeller	madxef	מַדחֵף (ז)
black box	kufsa ʃxora	קוּפסָה שחוֹרָה (נ)
yoke (control column)	'hege	הֶגֶה (ז)
fuel	'delek	דֶלֶק (ז)
safety card	hora'ot betixut	הוֹרָאוֹת בְּטִיחוּת (נ״ר)
oxygen mask	masexat xamtsan	מַסֵיכַת חַמצָן (נ)
uniform	madim	מַדִים (ז״ר)
life vest	xagorat hatsala	חֲגוֹרַת הַצָלָה (נ)
parachute	mitsnax	מִצנָח (ז)
takeoff	hamra'a	הַמרָאָה (נ)
to take off (vi)	lehamri	לְהַמרִיא
runway	maslul hamra'a	מַסלוּל הַמרָאָה (ז)
visibility	re'ut	רְאוּת (נ)
flight (act of flying)	tisa	טִיסָה (נ)
altitude	'gova	גוֹבַה (ז)
air pocket	kis avir	כִּיס אֲוִויר (ז)
seat	moʃav	מוֹשָב (ז)
headphones	ozniyot	אוֹזנִיוֹת (נ״ר)

folding tray (tray table)	magaʃ mitkapel	מַגָשׁ מִתקַפֵּל (ז)
airplane window	tsohar	צוֹהַר (ז)
aisle	ma'avar	מַעֲבָר (ז)

106. Train

train	ra'kevet	רַכֶּבֶת (נ)
commuter train	ra'kevet parvarim	רַכֶּבֶת פַּרבָרִים (נ)
express train	ra'kevet mehira	רַכֶּבֶת מְהִירָה (נ)
diesel locomotive	katar 'dizel	קַטָר דִיזָל (ז)
steam locomotive	katar	קַטָר (ז)
passenger car	karon	קָרוֹן (ז)
dining car	kron mis'ada	קָרוֹן מִסעָדָה (ז)
rails	mesilot	מְסִילוֹת (נ״ר)
railroad	mesilat barzel	מְסִילַת בַּרזֶל (נ)
railway tie	'eden	אֶדֶן (ז)
platform (railway ~)	ratsif	רָצִיף (ז)
track (~ 1, 2, etc.)	mesila	מְסִילָה (נ)
semaphore	ramzor	רַמזוֹר (ז)
station	taχana	תַחֲנָה (נ)
engineer (train driver)	nahag ra'kevet	נַהָג רַכֶּבֶת (ז)
porter (of luggage)	sabal	סַבָּל (ז)
car attendant	sadran ra'kevet	סַדרָן רַכֶּבֶת (ז)
passenger	no'se'a	נוֹסֵעַ (ז)
conductor (ticket inspector)	bodek	בּוֹדֵק (ז)
corridor (in train)	prozdor	פּרוֹזדוֹר (ז)
emergency brake	ma'atsar χirum	מַעֲצַר חִירוּם (ז)
compartment	ta	תָא (ז)
berth	dargaʃ	דַרגָשׁ (ז)
upper berth	dargaʃ elyon	דַרגָשׁ עֶליוֹן (ז)
lower berth	dargaʃ taχton	דַרגָשׁ תַחתוֹן (ז)
bed linen, bedding	matsa'im	מַצָעִים (ז״ר)
ticket	kartis	כַּרטִיס (ז)
schedule	'luaχ zmanim	לוּחַ זמַנִים (ז)
information display	'ʃelet meida	שֶׁלֶט מֵידַע (ז)
to leave, to depart	latset	לָצֵאת
departure (of train)	yetsi'a	יְצִיאָה (נ)
to arrive (ab. train)	leha'gi'a	לְהַגִיעַ
arrival	haga'a	הַגָעָה (נ)
to arrive by train	leha'gi'a bera'kevet	לְהַגִיעַ בְּרַכֶּבֶת
to get on the train	la'alot lera'kevet	לַעֲלוֹת לְרַכֶּבֶת

to get off the train	la'redet mehara'kevet	לָרֶדֶת מֵהָרַכֶּבֶת
train wreck	hitraskut	הִתְרַסְקוּת (נ)
to derail (vi)	la'redet mipasei ra'kevet	לָרֶדֶת מִפַּסֵי רַכֶּבֶת
steam locomotive	katar	קַטָּר (ז)
stoker, fireman	masik	מַסִּיק (ז)
firebox	kivʃan	כִּבְשָׁן (ז)
coal	peχam	פֶּחָם (ז)

107. Ship

ship	sfina	סְפִינָה (נ)
vessel	sfina	סְפִינָה (נ)
steamship	oniyat kitor	אוֹנִיַּית קִיטוֹר (נ)
riverboat	sfinat nahar	סְפִינַת נָהָר (נ)
cruise ship	oniyat ta'anugot	אוֹנִיַּית תַּעֲנוּגוֹת (נ)
cruiser	sa'yeret	סַיֶּרֶת (נ)
yacht	'yaχta	יַכְטָה (נ)
tugboat	go'reret	גוֹרֶרֶת (נ)
barge	arba	אַרְבָּה (נ)
ferry	ma'a'boret	מַעֲבּוֹרֶת (נ)
sailing ship	sfinat mifras	סְפִינַת מִפְרָשׂ (נ)
brigantine	briganit	בְּרִיגָּנִית (נ)
ice breaker	ʃo'veret 'keraχ	שׁוֹבֶרֶת קֶרַח (נ)
submarine	tso'lelet	צוֹלֶלֶת (נ)
boat (flat-bottomed ~)	sira	סִירָה (נ)
dinghy	sira	סִירָה (נ)
lifeboat	sirat hatsala	סִירַת הַצָּלָה (נ)
motorboat	sirat ma'no'a	סִירַת מָנוֹעַ (נ)
captain	rav χovel	רַב־חוֹבֵל (ז)
seaman	malaχ	מַלָּח (ז)
sailor	yamai	יַמַּאי (ז)
crew	'tsevet	צֶוֶת (ז)
boatswain	rav malaχim	רַב־מַלָּחִים (ז)
ship's boy	'na'ar sipun	נַעַר סִיפּוּן (ז)
cook	tabaχ	טַבָּח (ז)
ship's doctor	rofe ha'oniya	רוֹפֵא הָאוֹנִיָּיה (ז)
deck	sipun	סִיפּוּן (ז)
mast	'toren	תּוֹרֶן (ז)
sail	mifras	מִפְרָשׂ (ז)
hold	'beten oniya	בֶּטֶן אוֹנִיָּיה (נ)
bow (prow)	χartom	חַרְטוֹם (ז)

stern	yarketei hasfina	יַרְכְּתֵי הַסְּפִינָה (ז״ר)
oar	maʃot	מָשׁוֹט (ז)
screw propeller	madxef	מַדְחֵף (ז)
cabin	ta	תָּא (ז)
wardroom	moʻadon ktsinim	מוֹעֲדוֹן קְצִינִים (ז)
engine room	xadar mexonot	חֲדַר מְכוֹנוֹת (ז)
bridge	ʻgeʃer hapikud	גֶּשֶׁר הַפִּיקוּד (ז)
radio room	ta alxutan	תָּא אַלְחוּטָן (ז)
wave (radio)	ʻteder	תֶּדֶר (ז)
logbook	yoman haʻoniya	יוֹמַן הָאוֹנִיָּה (ז)
spyglass	miʃkefet	מִשְׁקֶפֶת (נ)
bell	paʻamon	פַּעֲמוֹן (ז)
flag	ʻdegel	דֶּגֶל (ז)
hawser (mooring ~)	avot haʻoniya	עֲבוֹת הָאוֹנִיָּה (נ)
knot (bowline, etc.)	ʻkeʃer	קֶשֶׁר (ז)
deckrails	maʻake hasipun	מַעֲקֵה הַסִּיפּוּן (ז)
gangway	ʻkeveʃ	כֶּבֶשׁ (ז)
anchor	ʻogen	עוֹגֶן (ז)
to weigh anchor	leharim ʻogen	לְהָרִים עוֹגֶן
to drop anchor	laʻagon	לַעֲגוֹן
anchor chain	ʃarʼʃeret haʻogen	שַׁרְשֶׁרֶת הָעוֹגֶן (נ)
port (harbor)	namal	נָמֵל (ז)
quay, wharf	ʻmezax	מֶזַח (ז)
to berth (moor)	laʻagon	לַעֲגוֹן
to cast off	lehaflig	לְהַפְלִיג
trip, voyage	masa, tiyul	מַסָּע (ז), טִיּוּל (ז)
cruise (sea trip)	ʻʃayit	שַׁיִט (ז)
course (route)	kivun	כִּיווּן (ז)
route (itinerary)	nativ	נָתִיב (ז)
fairway (safe water channel)	nativ ʻʃayit	נְתִיב שַׁיִט (ז)
shallows	sirton	שִׂרְטוֹן (ז)
to run aground	laʻalot al hasirton	לַעֲלוֹת עַל הַשִּׂרְטוֹן
storm	sufa	סוּפָה (נ)
signal	ot	אוֹת (ז)
to sink (vi)	litʻboʻa	לִטְבּוֹעַ
Man overboard!	adam baʻmayim!	אָדָם בַּמַּיִם!
SOS (distress signal)	kriʼat hatsala	קְרִיאַת הַצָּלָה
ring buoy	galgal hatsala	גַּלְגַּל הַצָּלָה (ז)

108. Airport

airport	nemal te'ufa	נְמַל תְעוּפָה (ז)
airplane	matos	מָטוֹס (ז)
airline	xevrat te'ufa	חֶבְרַת תְעוּפָה (נ)
air traffic controller	bakar tisa	בַּקָר טִיסָה (ז)
departure	hamra'a	הַמְרָאָה (נ)
arrival	nexita	נְחִיתָה (נ)
to arrive (by plane)	leha'gi'a betisa	לְהַגִיעַ בְּטִיסָה
departure time	zman hamra'a	זְמַן הַמְרָאָה (ז)
arrival time	zman nexita	זְמַן נְחִיתָה (ז)
to be delayed	lehit'akev	לְהִתְעַכֵּב
flight delay	ikuv hatisa	עִיכּוּב הַטִיסָה (ז)
information board	'luax meida	לוּחַ מֵידָע (ז)
information	meida	מֵידָע (ז)
to announce (vt)	leho'dia	לְהוֹדִיעַ
flight (e.g., next ~)	tisa	טִיסָה (נ)
customs	'mexes	מֶכֶס (ז)
customs officer	pakid 'mexes	פָּקִיד מֶכֶס (ז)
customs declaration	hatsharat mexes	הַצהָרַת מֶכֶס (נ)
to fill out (vt)	lemale	לְמַלֵא
to fill out the declaration	lemale 'tofes hatshara	לְמַלֵא טוֹפֶס הַצהָרָה
passport control	bdikat darkonim	בְּדִיקַת דַרכּוֹנִים (נ)
luggage	kvuda	כְּבוּדָה (נ)
hand luggage	kvudat yad	כְּבוּדַת יָד (נ)
luggage cart	eglat kvuda	עֶגלַת כְּבוּדָה (נ)
landing	nexita	נְחִיתָה (נ)
landing strip	maslul nexita	מַסלוּל נְחִיתָה (ז)
to land (vi)	linxot	לִנחוֹת
airstairs	'keveʃ	כֶּבֶשׁ (ז)
check-in	tʃek in	צֶ'ק אִין (ז)
check-in counter	dalpak tʃek in	דַלפָּק צֶ'ק אִין (ז)
to check-in (vi)	leva'tse'a tʃek in	לְבַצֵעַ צֶ'ק אִין
boarding pass	kartis aliya lematos	כַּרטִיס עֲלִיָה לְמָטוֹס (ז)
departure gate	'ʃa'ar yetsi'a	שַעַר יְצִיאָה (ז)
transit	ma'avar	מַעֲבָר (ז)
to wait (vt)	lehamtin	לְהַמתִין
departure lounge	traklin tisa	טרַקלִין טִיסָה (ז)
to see off	lelavot	לְלַוּוֹת
to say goodbye	lomar lehitra'ot	לוֹמַר לְהִתְרָאוֹת

T&P Books. Hebrew vocabulary for English speakers - 5000 words

Life events

109. Holidays. Event

celebration, holiday	xagiga	חֲגִיגָה (נ)
national day	xag le'umi	חַג לְאוּמִי (ז)
public holiday	yom xag	יוֹם חַג (ז)
to commemorate (vt)	laxgog	לַחגוֹג
event (happening)	hitraxafut	הִתרַחֲשוּת (נ)
event (organized activity)	ei'ru'a	אֵירוּעַ (ז)
banquet (party)	se'uda xagigit	סְעוּדָה חֲגִיגִית (נ)
reception (formal party)	ei'ruax	אֵירוּחַ (ז)
feast	mifte	מִשתֶה (ז)
anniversary	yom hafana	יוֹם הַשָנָה (ז)
jubilee	xag hayovel	חַג הַיוֹבֵל (ז)
to celebrate (vt)	laxgog	לַחגוֹג
New Year	fana xadafa	שָנָה חָדָשָה (נ)
Happy New Year!	fana tova!	שָנָה טוֹבָה!
Santa Claus	'santa 'kla'us	סַנטָה קלָאוּס
Christmas	xag hamolad	חַג הַמוֹלָד (ז)
Merry Christmas!	xag hamolad sa'meax!	חַג הַמוֹלָד שָׂמֵחַ!
Christmas tree	ets xag hamolad	עֵץ חַג הַמוֹלָד (ז)
fireworks (fireworks show)	zikukim	זִיקוּקִים (ז״ר)
wedding	xatuna	חֲתוּנָה (נ)
groom	xatan	חָתָן (ז)
bride	kala	כַּלָה (נ)
to invite (vt)	lehazmin	לְהַזמִין
invitation card	hazmana	הַזמָנָה (נ)
guest	o'reax	אוֹרֵחַ (ז)
to visit	levaker	לְבַקֵר
(~ your parents, etc.)		
to meet the guests	lekabel orxim	לְקַבֵּל אוֹרחִים
gift, present	matana	מַתָנָה (נ)
to give (sth as present)	latet matana	לָתֵת מַתָנָה
to receive gifts	lekabel matanot	לְקַבֵּל מַתָנוֹת
bouquet (of flowers)	zer	זֵר (ז)
congratulations	braxa	בּרָכָה (נ)
to congratulate (vt)	levarex	לְבָרֵך

119

greeting card	kartis braxa	כַּרְטִיס בְּרָכָה (ז)
to send a postcard	lifloax gluya	לִשׁלוֹחַ גלוּיָה
to get a postcard	lekabel gluya	לְקַבֵּל גלוּיָה
toast	leharim kosit	לְהָרִים כּוֹסִית
to offer (a drink, etc.)	lexabed	לְכַבֵּד
champagne	ʃam'panya	שַׁמפַּניָה (נ)
to enjoy oneself	lehanot	לֵיהָנוֹת
merriment (gaiety)	alitsut	עַלִיצוּת (נ)
joy (emotion)	simxa	שִׂמחָה (נ)
dance	rikud	רִיקוּד (ז)
to dance (vi, vt)	lirkod	לִרקוֹד
waltz	vals	וַלס (ז)
tango	'tango	טַנגוֹ (ז)

110. Funerals. Burial

cemetery	beit kvarot	בֵּית קבָרוֹת (ז)
grave, tomb	'kever	קֶבֶר (ז)
cross	tslav	צלָב (ז)
gravestone	matseva	מַצֵבָה (נ)
fence	gader	גָדֵר (נ)
chapel	beit tfila	בֵּית תפִילָה (ז)
death	'mavet	מָווֶת (ז)
to die (vi)	lamut	לָמוּת
the deceased	niftar	נִפטָר (ז)
mourning	'evel	אֵבֶל (ז)
to bury (vt)	likbor	לִקבּוֹר
funeral home	beit levayot	בֵּית לוָויוֹת (ז)
funeral	levaya	לוָויָה (נ)
wreath	zer	זֵר (ז)
casket, coffin	aron metim	אֲרוֹן מֵתִים (ז)
hearse	kron hamet	קרוֹן הַמֵת (ז)
shroud	taxriximmm	תַברִיכִים (ז״ר)
funeral procession	tahaluxat 'evel	תַהֲלוּכַת אֵבֶל (נ)
funerary urn	kad 'efer	כַּד אֵפֶר (ז)
crematory	misrafa	מִשׂרָפָה (נ)
obituary	moda'at 'evel	מוֹדָעַת אֵבֶל (נ)
to cry (weep)	livkot	לִבכּוֹת
to sob (vi)	lehitya'peax	לְהִתייַפַּח

111. War. Soldiers

platoon	maxlaka	מַחְלָקָה (נ)
company	pluga	פְּלוּגָה (נ)
regiment	xativa	חֲטִיבָה (נ)
army	tsava	צָבָא (ז)
division	ugda	אוּגְדָּה (נ)
section, squad	kita	כִּיתָה (נ)
host (army)	'xayil	חַיִל (ז)
soldier	xayal	חַיָּל (ז)
officer	katsin	קָצִין (ז)
private	turai	טוּרַאי (ז)
sergeant	samal	סַמָּל (ז)
lieutenant	'segen	סֶגֶן (ז)
captain	'seren	סֶרֶן (ז)
major	rav 'seren	רַב־סֶרֶן (ז)
colonel	aluf miʃne	אַלּוּף מִשְׁנֶה (ז)
general	aluf	אַלּוּף (ז)
sailor	yamai	יַמַּאי (ז)
captain	rav xovel	רַב־חוֹבֵל (ז)
boatswain	rav malaxim	רַב־מַלָּחִים (ז)
artilleryman	totxan	תּוֹתְחָן (ז)
paratrooper	tsanxan	צַנְחָן (ז)
pilot	tayas	טַיָּס (ז)
navigator	navat	נַוָּט (ז)
mechanic	mexonai	מְכוֹנַאי (ז)
pioneer (sapper)	xablan	חַבְּלָן (ז)
parachutist	tsanxan	צַנְחָן (ז)
reconnaissance scout	iʃ modi'in kravi	אִישׁ מוֹדִיעִין קְרָבִי (ז)
sniper	tsalaf	צַלָּף (ז)
patrol (group)	siyur	סִיּוּר (ז)
to patrol (vt)	lefatrel	לְפַטְרֵל
sentry, guard	zakif	זָקִיף (ז)
warrior	loxem	לוֹחֵם (ז)
patriot	patriyot	פַּטְרִיּוֹט (ז)
hero	gibor	גִּיבּוֹר (ז)
heroine	gibora	גִּיבּוֹרָה (נ)
traitor	boged	בּוֹגֵד (ז)
to betray (vt)	livgod	לִבְגוֹד
deserter	arik	עָרִיק (ז)
to desert (vi)	la'arok	לַעֲרוֹק
mercenary	sxir 'xerev	שְׂכִיר חֶרֶב (ז)

| recruit | tiron | טִירוֹן (ז) |
| volunteer | mitnadev | מִתנַדֵב (ז) |

dead (n)	harug	הָרוּג (ז)
wounded (n)	pa'tsu'a	פָּצוּעַ (ז)
prisoner of war	ʃavui	שָבוּי (ז)

112. War. Military actions. Part 1

war	milxama	מִלחָמָה (נ)
to be at war	lehilaxem	לְהִילָחֵם
civil war	mil'xemet ezraxim	מִלחֶמֶת אֶזרָחִים (נ)

treacherously (adv)	bogdani	בּוֹגדָנִי
declaration of war	haxrazat milxama	הַכרָזַת מִלחָמָה (נ)
to declare (~ war)	lehaxriz	לְהַכרִיז
aggression	tokfanut	תוֹקפָנוּת (נ)
to attack (invade)	litkof	לִתקוֹף

to invade (vt)	lixboʃ	לִכבּוֹש
invader	koveʃ	כּוֹבֵש (ז)
conqueror	koveʃ	כּוֹבֵש (ז)

defense	hagana	הֲגָנָה (נ)
to defend (a country, etc.)	lehagen al	לְהָגֵן עַל
to defend (against …)	lehitgonen	לְהִתגוֹנֵן

enemy	oyev	אוֹיֵב (ז)
foe, adversary	yariv	יָרִיב (ז)
enemy (as adj)	ʃel oyev	שֶל אוֹיֵב

| strategy | astra'tegya | אַסטרָטֶגיָה (נ) |
| tactics | 'taktika | טַקטִיקָה (נ) |

order	pkuda	פְּקוּדָה (נ)
command (order)	pkuda	פְּקוּדָה (נ)
to order (vt)	lifkod	לִפקוֹד
mission	mesima	מְשִׂימָה (נ)
secret (adj)	sodi	סוֹדִי

| battle | ma'araxa | מַעֲרָכָה (נ) |
| combat | krav | קרָב (ז) |

attack	hatkafa	הַתקָפָה (נ)
charge (assault)	hista'arut	הִסתָעֲרוּת (נ)
to storm (vt)	lehista'er	לְהִסתָעֵר
siege (to be under ~)	matsor	מָצוֹר (ז)

| offensive (n) | mitkafa | מִתקָפָה (נ) |
| to go on the offensive | latset lemitkafa | לָצֵאת לְמִתקָפָה |

retreat	nesiga	נְסִיגָה (נ)
to retreat (vi)	la'seget	לָסֶגֶת
encirclement	kitur	כִּיתוּר (ז)
to encircle (vt)	leχater	לְכַתֵּר
bombing (by aircraft)	haftsatsa	הַפְצָצָה (נ)
to drop a bomb	lehatil ptsatsa	לְהָטִיל פְּצָצָה
to bomb (vt)	lehaftsits	לְהַפְצִיץ
explosion	pitsuts	פִּיצוּץ (ז)
shot	yeriya	יְרִיָה (נ)
to fire (~ a shot)	lirot	לִירוֹת
firing (burst of ~)	'yeri	יְרִי (ז)
to aim (to point a weapon)	leχaven 'nefek	לְכַוֵון נֶשֶק
to point (a gun)	leχaven	לְכַוֵון
to hit (the target)	lik'lo'a	לִקְלוֹעַ
to sink (~ a ship)	lehat'bi'a	לְהַטְבִּיעַ
hole (in a ship)	pirtsa	פִּרְצָה (נ)
to founder, to sink (vi)	lit'bo'a	לִטְבּוֹעַ
front (war ~)	χazit	חָזִית (נ)
evacuation	pinui	פִּינוּי (ז)
to evacuate (vt)	lefanot	לְפַנוֹת
trench	te'ala	תְעָלָה (נ)
barbwire	'tayil dokrani	תַיִל דוֹקְרָנִי (ז)
barrier (anti tank ~)	maχsom	מַחְסוֹם (ז)
watchtower	migdal ʃmira	מִגְדַל שמִירָה (ז)
military hospital	beit χolim tsva'i	בֵּית חוֹלִים צְבָאִי (ז)
to wound (vt)	lif'tso'a	לִפְצוֹעַ
wound	'petsa	פֶּצַע (ז)
wounded (n)	pa'tsu'a	פָּצוּעַ (ז)
to be wounded	lehipatsa	לְהִיפָּצַע
serious (wound)	kaʃe	קָשֶה

113. War. Military actions. Part 2

captivity	'ʃevi	שְבִי (ז)
to take captive	la'kaχat be'ʃevi	לָקַחַת בְּשֶבְי
to be held captive	lihyot be'ʃevi	לִהיוֹת בְּשֶבְי
to be taken captive	lipol be'ʃevi	לִיפּוֹל בַּשֶבְי
concentration camp	maχane rikuz	מַחֲנֵה רִיכּוּז (ז)
prisoner of war	ʃavui	שָבוּי (ז)
to escape (vi)	liv'roaχ	לִברוֹחַ
to betray (vt)	livgod	לִבגוֹד

betrayer	boged	בּוֹגֵד (ז)
betrayal	bgida	בְּגִידָה (נ)
to execute (by firing squad)	lehotsi la'horeg	לְהוֹצִיא לַהוֹרֵג
execution (by firing squad)	hotsa'a le'horeg	הוֹצָאָה לַהוֹרֵג (נ)
equipment (military gear)	tsiyud	צִיוּד (ז)
shoulder board	ko'tefet	כּוֹתֶפֶת (נ)
gas mask	maseχat 'abaχ	מָסֵיכַת אַבָּ"ך (נ)
field radio	maχʃir 'keʃer	מַכְשִׁיר קֶשֶׁר (ז)
cipher, code	'tsofen	צוֹפֶן (ז)
secrecy	χaʃa'iut	חֲשָׁאִיוּת (נ)
password	sisma	סִיסְמָה (נ)
land mine	mokeʃ	מוֹקֵשׁ (ז)
to mine (road, etc.)	lemakeʃ	לְמַקֵשׁ
minefield	sde mokʃim	שְׂדֵה מוֹקְשִׁים (ז)
air-raid warning	az'aka	אַזְעָקָה (נ)
alarm (alert signal)	az'aka	אַזְעָקָה (נ)
signal	ot	אוֹת (ז)
signal flare	zikuk az'aka	זִיקוּק אַזְעָקָה (ז)
headquarters	mifkada	מִפְקָדָה (נ)
reconnaissance	isuf modi'in	אִיסוּף מוֹדִיעִין (ז)
situation	matsav	מַצָב (ז)
report	doχ	דוֹ"ח (ז)
ambush	ma'arav	מַאֲרָב (ז)
reinforcement (of army)	tig'boret	תִגְבּוֹרֶת (נ)
target	matara	מַטָרָה (נ)
proving ground	sde imunim	שְׂדֵה אִימוּנִים (ז)
military exercise	timronim	תִמְרוֹנִים (ז"ר)
panic	behala	בֶּהָלָה (נ)
devastation	'heres	הֶרֶס (ז)
destruction, ruins	harisot	הֲרִיסוֹת (נ"ר)
to destroy (vt)	laharos	לַהֲרוֹס
to survive (vi, vt)	lisrod	לִשְׂרוֹד
to disarm (vt)	lifrok mi'neʃek	לִפְרוֹק מִנֶשֶׁק
to handle (~ a gun)	lehiʃtameʃ be...	לְהִשְׁתַמֵשׁ בְּ...
Attention!	amod dom!	עֲמוֹד דוֹם!
At ease!	amod 'noaχ!	עֲמוֹד נוֹחַ!
act of courage	ma'ase gvura	מַעֲשֵׂה גְבוּרָה (ז)
oath (vow)	ʃvu'a	שְׁבוּעָה (נ)
to swear (an oath)	lehiʃava	לְהִישָׁבַע
decoration (medal, etc.)	itur	עִיטוּר (ז)

to award (give medal to)	leha'anik	לְהַעֲנִיק
medal	me'dalya	מֶדַלְיָה (נ)
order (e.g., ~ of Merit)	ot hitstainut	אוֹת הִצְטַיְינוּת (ז)
victory	nitsaxon	נִיצָחוֹן (ז)
defeat	tvusa	תבוּסָה (נ)
armistice	hafsakat eʃ	הַפְסָקַת אֵשׁ (נ)
standard (battle flag)	'degel	דֶגֶל (ז)
glory (honor, fame)	tehila	תְהִילָה (נ)
parade	mits'ad	מִצְעָד (ז)
to march (on parade)	lits'od	לִצְעוֹד

114. Weapons

weapons	'neʃek	נֶשֶׁק (ז)
firearms	'neʃek xam	נֶשֶׁק חַם (ז)
cold weapons (knives, etc.)	'neʃek kar	נֶשֶׁק קַר (ז)
chemical weapons	'neʃek 'ximi	נֶשֶׁק כִימִי (ז)
nuclear (adj)	gar'ini	גַרְעִינִי
nuclear weapons	'neʃek gar'ini	נֶשֶׁק גַרְעִינִי (ז)
bomb	ptsatsa	פְּצָצָה (נ)
atomic bomb	ptsatsa a'tomit	פְּצָצָה אָטוֹמִית (נ)
pistol (gun)	ekdax	אֶקְדָח (ז)
rifle	rove	רוֹבֶה (ז)
submachine gun	tat mak'le'a	תַת־מַקְלֵעַ (ז)
machine gun	mak'le'a	מַקְלֵעַ (ז)
muzzle	kane	קָנֶה (ז)
barrel	kane	קָנֶה (ז)
caliber	ka'liber	קָלִיבֶּר (ז)
trigger	'hedek	הֶדֶק (ז)
sight (aiming device)	ka'venet	כַּוֶונֶת (נ)
magazine	maxsanit	מַחְסָנִית (נ)
butt (shoulder stock)	kat	קַת (נ)
hand grenade	rimon	רִימוֹן (ז)
explosive	'xomer 'nefets	חוֹמֶר נֶפֶץ (ז)
bullet	ka'li'a	קָלִיעַ (ז)
cartridge	kadur	כַּדוּר (ז)
charge	te'ina	טְעִינָה (נ)
ammunition	tax'moʃet	תַחְמוֹשֶׁת (נ)
bomber (aircraft)	maftsits	מַפְצִיץ (ז)
fighter	metos krav	מְטוֹס קְרָב (ז)

helicopter	masok	מָסוֹק (ז)
anti-aircraft gun	totaχ 'neged metosim	תּוֹתָח נֶגֶד מְטוֹסִים (ז)
tank	tank	טַנק (ז)
tank gun	totaχ	תּוֹתָח (ז)

artillery	arti'lerya	אַרטִילֶריָה (נ)
gun (cannon, howitzer)	totaχ	תּוֹתָח (ז)
to lay (a gun)	leχaven	לְכַוֵון

shell (projectile)	pagaz	פָּגָז (ז)
mortar bomb	ptsatsat margema	פְּצָצַת מַרגֵמָה (נ)
mortar	margema	מַרגֵמָה (נ)
splinter (shell fragment)	resis	רְסִיס (ז)

submarine	tso'lelet	צוֹלֶלֶת (נ)
torpedo	tor'pedo	טוֹרפֶּדוֹ (ז)
missile	til	טִיל (ז)

to load (gun)	lit'on	לִטעוֹן
to shoot (vi)	lirot	לִירוֹת
to point at (the cannon)	leχaven	לְכַוֵון
bayonet	kidon	כִּידוֹן (ז)

rapier	'χerev	חֶרֶב (נ)
saber (e.g., cavalry ~)	'χerev paraʃim	חֶרֶב פָּרָשִים (ז)
spear (weapon)	χanit	חֲנִית (נ)
bow	'keʃet	קֶשֶת (נ)
arrow	χets	חֵץ (ז)
musket	musket	מוּסקֶט (ז)
crossbow	'keʃet metsu'levet	קֶשֶת מְצוּלֶבֶת (נ)

115. Ancient people

primitive (prehistoric)	kadmon	קַדמוֹן
prehistoric (adj)	prehis'tori	פְּרֶהִיסטוֹרִי
ancient (~ civilization)	atik	עָתִיק

Stone Age	idan ha''even	עִידָן הָאֶבֶן (ז)
Bronze Age	idan ha'arad	עִידָן הָאָרָד (ז)
Ice Age	idan ha'keraχ	עִידָן הַקֶרַח (ז)

tribe	'ʃevet	שֶבֶט (ז)
cannibal	oχel adam	אוֹכֵל אָדָם (ז)
hunter	tsayad	צַיָיד (ז)
to hunt (vi, vt)	latsud	לָצוּד
mammoth	ma'muta	מָמוּתָה (נ)

cave	me'ara	מְעָרָה (נ)
fire	eʃ	אֵש (נ)
campfire	medura	מְדוּרָה (נ)

cave painting	pet'roglif	פֶּטְרוֹגְלִיף (ז)
tool (e.g., stone ax)	kli	כְּלִי (ז)
spear	χanit	חָנִית (נ)
stone ax	garzen ha'even	גַרְזֶן הָאֶבֶן (ז)
to be at war	lehilaχem	לְהִילָחֵם
to domesticate (vt)	levayet	לְבַיֵית

idol	'pesel	פֶּסֶל (ז)
to worship (vt)	la'avod et	לַעֲבוֹד אֶת
superstition	emuna tfela	אֱמוּנָה תְפֵלָה (נ)
rite	'tekes	טֶקֶס (ז)

evolution	evo'lutsya	אֵבוֹלוּצְיָה (נ)
development	hitpatχut	הִתפַּתחוּת (נ)
disappearance (extinction)	he'almut	הֵיעָלְמוּת (נ)
to adapt oneself	lehistagel	לְהִסתַגֵל

archeology	arχe'o'logya	אַרכֵיאוֹלוֹגיָה (נ)
archeologist	arχe'olog	אַרכֵיאוֹלוֹג (ז)
archeological (adj)	arχe'o'logi	אַרכֵיאוֹלוֹגִי

excavation site	atar χafirot	אָתַר חָפִירוֹת (ז)
excavations	χafirot	חָפִירוֹת (נ״ר)
find (object)	mimtsa	מִמצָא (ז)
fragment	resis	רְסִיס (ז)

116. Middle Ages

people (ethnic group)	am	עַם (ז)
peoples	amim	עַמִים (ז״ר)
tribe	'ʃevet	שֵבֶט (ז)
tribes	ʃvatim	שבָטִים (ז״ר)

barbarians	bar'barim	בַּרבָּרִים (ז״ר)
Gauls	'galim	גָאלִים (ז״ר)
Goths	'gotim	גוֹתִים (ז״ר)
Slavs	'slavim	סלָאבִים (ז״ר)
Vikings	'vikingim	וִיקִינגִים (ז״ר)

Romans	roma'im	רוֹמָאִים (ז״ר)
Roman (adj)	'romi	רוֹמִי

Byzantines	bi'zantim	בִּיזַנטִים (ז״ר)
Byzantium	bizantion, bizants	בִּיזַנטיוֹן, בִּיזַנץ (נ)
Byzantine (adj)	bi'zanti	בִּיזַנטִי

emperor	keisar	קֵיסָר (ז)
leader, chief (tribal ~)	manhig	מַנהִיג (ז)
powerful (~ king)	rav 'koaχ	רַב־כּוֹחַ
king	'meleχ	מֶלֶך (ז)

ruler (sovereign)	ʃalit	שָׁלִיט (ז)
knight	abir	אַבִּיר (ז)
feudal lord	fe'odal	פֵיאוֹדָל (ז)
feudal (adj)	fe'o'dali	פֵיאוֹדָלִי
vassal	vasal	וַסָל (ז)
duke	dukas	דוּכָּס (ז)
earl	rozen	רוֹזֵן (ז)
baron	baron	בָּרוֹן (ז)
bishop	'biʃof	בִּישׁוֹף (ז)
armor	ʃiryon	שִׁרְיוֹן (ז)
shield	magen	מָגֵן (ז)
sword	'xerev	חֶרֶב (נ)
visor	magen panim	מָגֵן פָּנִים (ז)
chainmail	ʃiryon kaskasim	שִׁרְיוֹן קַשְׂקַשִׂים (ז)
Crusade	masa tslav	מַסָע צְלָב (ז)
crusader	tsalban	צַלְבָּן (ז)
territory	'ʃetax	שֶׁטַח (ז)
to attack (invade)	litkof	לִתְקוֹף
to conquer (vt)	lixboʃ	לִכְבּוֹשׁ
to occupy (invade)	lehiʃtalet	לְהִשְׁתַלֵט
siege (to be under ~)	matsor	מָצוֹר (ז)
besieged (adj)	natsur	נָצוּר
to besiege (vt)	latsur	לָצוּר
inquisition	inkvi'zitsya	אִינְקְווִיזִיצְיָה (נ)
inquisitor	inkvi'zitor	אִינְקְווִיזִיטוֹר (ז)
torture	inui	עִינוּי (ז)
cruel (adj)	axzari	אַכְזָרִי
heretic	kofer	כּוֹפֵר (ז)
heresy	kfira	כְּפִירָה (נ)
seafaring	haflaga bayam	הַפְלָגָה בַּיָם (נ)
pirate	ʃoded yam	שׁוֹדֵד יָם (ז)
piracy	pi'ratiyut	פִּירָטִיוּת (נ)
boarding (attack)	la'alot al	לַעֲלוֹת עַל
loot, booty	ʃalal	שָׁלָל (ז)
treasures	otsarot	אוֹצָרוֹת (ז"ר)
discovery	taglit	תַגְלִית (נ)
to discover (new land, etc.)	legalot	לְגַלוֹת
expedition	miʃlaxat	מִשְׁלַחַת (נ)
musketeer	musketer	מוּסְקֶטֶר (ז)
cardinal	xaʃman	חַשְׁמָן (ז)
heraldry	he'raldika	הֶרַלְדִיקָה (נ)
heraldic (adj)	he'raldi	הֶרַלְדִי

117. Leader. Chief. Authorities

king	'melex	מֶלֶךְ (ז)
queen	malka	מַלְכָּה (נ)
royal (adj)	malxuti	מַלְכוּתִי
kingdom	mamlaxa	מַמְלָכָה (נ)
prince	nasix	נָסִיךְ (ז)
princess	nesixa	נְסִיכָה (נ)
president	nasi	נָשִׂיא (ז)
vice-president	sgan nasi	סגַן נָשִׂיא (ז)
senator	se'nator	סֶנָאטוֹר (ז)
monarch	'melex	מֶלֶךְ (ז)
ruler (sovereign)	ʃalit	שַׁלִיט (ז)
dictator	rodan	רוֹדָן (ז)
tyrant	aruts	עָרוּץ (ז)
magnate	eil hon	אֵיל הוֹן (ז)
director	menahel	מְנָהֵל (ז)
chief	menahel, roʃ	מְנָהֵל (ז), רֹאש (ז)
manager (director)	menahel	מְנָהֵל (ז)
boss	bos	בּוֹס (ז)
owner	'ba'al	בַּעַל (ז)
leader	manhig	מַנהִיג (ז)
head (~ of delegation)	roʃ	רֹאש (ז)
authorities	ʃiltonot	שִׁלטוֹנוֹת (ז״ר)
superiors	memunim	מְמוּנִים (ז״ר)
governor	moʃel	מוֹשֵׁל (ז)
consul	'konsul	קוֹנסוּל (ז)
diplomat	diplomat	דִיפּלוֹמָט (ז)
mayor	roʃ ha'ir	רֹאש הָעִיר (ז)
sheriff	ʃerif	שֶׁרִיף (ז)
emperor	keisar	קֵיסָר (ז)
tsar, czar	tsar	צָאר (ז)
pharaoh	par'o	פַּרעֹה (ז)
khan	xan	חָאן (ז)

118. Breaking the law. Criminals. Part 1

bandit	ʃoded	שׁוֹדֵד (ז)
crime	'peʃa	פֶּשַׁע (ז)
criminal (person)	po'ʃe'a	פּוֹשֵׁעַ (ז)
thief	ganav	גַנָב (ז)
to steal (vi, vt)	lignov	לִגנוֹב

stealing (larceny)	gneva	גְּנֵיבָה (נ)
theft	gneva	גְּנֵיבָה (נ)
to kidnap (vt)	laxatof	לַחֲטוֹף
kidnapping	xatifa	חֲטִיפָה (נ)
kidnapper	xotef	חוֹטֵף (ז)
ransom	'kofer	כּוֹפֶר (ז)
to demand ransom	lidroʃ 'kofer	לִדרוֹש כּוֹפֶר
to rob (vt)	liʃdod	לִשדוֹד
robbery	ʃod	שוֹד (ז)
robber	ʃoded	שוֹדֵד (ז)
to extort (vt)	lisxot	לִסחוֹט
extortionist	saxtan	סַחטָן (ז)
extortion	saxtanut	סַחטָנוּת (נ)
to murder, to kill	lir'tsoax	לִרצוֹחַ
murder	'retsax	רֶצַח (ז)
murderer	ro'tseax	רוֹצֵחַ (ז)
gunshot	yeriya	יְרִייָה (נ)
to fire (~ a shot)	lirot	לִירוֹת
to shoot to death	lirot la'mavet	לִירוֹת לַמָווֶת
to shoot (vi)	lirot	לִירוֹת
shooting	'yeri	יְרִי (ז)
incident (fight, etc.)	takrit	תַקרִית (נ)
fight, brawl	ktata	קטָטָה (נ)
Help!	ha'tsilu!	הַצִילוּ!
victim	nifga	נִפגָע (ז)
to damage (vt)	lekalkel	לְקַלקֵל
damage	'nezek	נֶזֶק (ז)
dead body, corpse	gufa	גוּפָה (נ)
grave (~ crime)	xamur	חָמוּר
to attack (vt)	litkof	לִתקוֹף
to beat (to hit)	lehakot	לְהַכּוֹת
to beat up	lehakot	לְהַכּוֹת
to take (rob of sth)	la'kaxat be'koax	לָקַחַת בְּכוֹחַ
to stab to death	lidkor le'mavet	לִדקוֹר לְמָווֶת
to maim (vt)	lehatil mum	לְהָטִיל מוּם
to wound (vt)	lif'tso‘a	לִפצוֹעַ
blackmail	saxtanut	סַחטָנוּת (נ)
to blackmail (vt)	lisxot	לִסחוֹט
blackmailer	saxtan	סַחטָן (ז)
protection racket	dmei xasut	דמֵי חָסוּת (ז״ר)
racketeer	gove xasut	גוֹבֶה חָסוּת (ז)

gangster	'gangster	גַּנְגְּסְטֶר (ז)
mafia, Mob	'mafya	מַאפְיָה (נ)
pickpocket	kayas	כַּיָּס (ז)
burglar	porets	פּוֹרֵץ (ז)
smuggling	havraxa	הַבְרָחָה (נ)
smuggler	mav'riax	מַבְרִיחַ (ז)
forgery	ziyuf	זִיּוּף (ז)
to forge (counterfeit)	lezayef	לְזַיֵּיף
fake (forged)	mezuyaf	מְזוּיָף

119. Breaking the law. Criminals. Part 2

rape	'ones	אוֹנֶס (ז)
to rape (vt)	le'enos	לֶאֱנוֹס
rapist	anas	אַנָּס (ז)
maniac	'manyak	מַנְיָאק (ז)
prostitute (fem.)	zona	זוֹנָה (נ)
prostitution	znut	זְנוּת (נ)
pimp	sarsur	סַרְסוּר (ז)
drug addict	narkoman	נַרְקוֹמָן (ז)
drug dealer	soxer samim	סוֹחֵר סַמִּים (ז)
to blow up (bomb)	lefotsets	לְפוֹצֵץ
explosion	pitsuts	פִּיצוּץ (ז)
to set fire	lehatsit	לְהַצִּית
arsonist	matsit	מַצִּית (ז)
terrorism	terorizm	טֶרוֹרִיזְם (ז)
terrorist	mexabel	מְחַבֵּל (ז)
hostage	ben aruba	בֶּן עֲרוּבָּה (ז)
to swindle (deceive)	lehonot	לְהוֹנוֹת
swindle, deception	hona'a	הוֹנָאָה (נ)
swindler	ramai	רַמַּאי (ז)
to bribe (vt)	lefaxed	לְשַׁחֵד
bribery	'foxad	שׁוֹחַד (ז)
bribe	'foxad	שׁוֹחַד (ז)
poison	'ra'al	רַעַל (ז)
to poison (vt)	lehar'il	לְהַרְעִיל
to poison oneself	lehar'il et atsmo	לְהַרְעִיל אֶת עַצְמוֹ
suicide (act)	hit'abdut	הִתְאַבְּדוּת (נ)
suicide (person)	mit'abed	מִתְאַבֵּד (ז)
to threaten (vt)	le'ayem	לְאַיֵּים

threat	iyum	אִיוּם (ז)
to make an attempt	lehitnakeʃ	לְהִתְנַקֵּשׁ
attempt (attack)	nisayon hitnakʃut	נִיסָיוֹן הִתְנַקְּשׁוּת (ז)

| to steal (a car) | lignov | לִגְנוֹב |
| to hijack (a plane) | laxatof matos | לַחֲטוֹף מָטוֹס |

| revenge | nekama | נְקָמָה (נ) |
| to avenge (get revenge) | linkom | לִנְקוֹם |

to torture (vt)	la'anot	לְעַנּוֹת
torture	inui	עִינוּי (ז)
to torment (vt)	leyaser	לְיַיסֵּר

pirate	ʃoded yam	שׁוֹדֵד יָם (ז)
hooligan	xuligan	חוּלִיגָאן (ז)
armed (adj)	mezuyan	מְזוּיָן
violence	alimut	אַלִּימוּת (נ)
illegal (unlawful)	'bilti le'gali	בִּלְתִי לָגָלִי

| spying (espionage) | rigul | רִיגוּל (ז) |
| to spy (vi) | leragel | לְרַגֵּל |

120. Police. Law. Part 1

| justice | 'tsedek | צֶדֶק (ז) |
| court (see you in ~) | beit miʃpat | בֵּית מִשׁפָּט (ז) |

judge	ʃofet	שׁוֹפֵט (ז)
jurors	muʃba'im	מוּשׁבָּעִים (ז״ר)
jury trial	xaver muʃba'im	חָבֵר מוּשׁבָּעִים (ז)
to judge (vt)	liʃpot	לִשׁפּוֹט

lawyer, attorney	orex din	עוֹרֵךְ דִין (ז)
defendant	omed lemiʃpat	עוֹמֵד לְמִשׁפָּט (ז)
dock	safsal ne'eʃamim	סַפסָל נֶאֱשָׁמִים (ז)

| charge | ha'aʃama | הַאֲשָׁמָה (נ) |
| accused | ne'eʃam | נֶאֱשָׁם (ז) |

| sentence | gzar din | גזַר דִין (ז) |
| to sentence (vt) | lifsok | לִפסוֹק |

guilty (culprit)	aʃem	אָשֵׁם (ז)
to punish (vt)	leha'aniʃ	לְהַעֲנִישׁ
punishment	'oneʃ	עוֹנֶשׁ (ז)

fine (penalty)	knas	קנָס (ז)
life imprisonment	ma'asar olam	מַאֲסַר עוֹלָם (ז)
death penalty	'oneʃ 'mavet	עוֹנֶשׁ מָווֶת (ז)

electric chair	kise xaʃmali	כִּיסֵא חַשְׁמַלִי (ז)
gallows	gardom	גַרדוֹם (ז)
to execute (vt)	lehotsi la'horeg	לְהוֹצִיא לַהוֹרֶג
execution	hatsa'a le'horeg	הוֹצָאָה לַהוֹרֶג (נ)
prison, jail	beit 'sohar	בֵּית סוֹהַר (ז)
cell	ta	תָּא (ז)
escort	miʃmar livui	מִשמָר לִיווּי (ז)
prison guard	soher	סוֹהַר (ז)
prisoner	asir	אָסִיר (ז)
handcuffs	azikim	אֲזִיקִים (ז"ר)
to handcuff (vt)	lixbol be'azikim	לִכבּוֹל בָּאֲזִיקִים
prison break	brixa	בּרִיחָה (נ)
to break out (vi)	liv'roax	לִברוֹחַ
to disappear (vi)	lehe'alem	לְהֵיעָלֵם
to release (from prison)	leʃaxrer	לְשַחרֵר
amnesty	xanina	חֲנִינָה (נ)
police	miʃtara	מִשטָרָה (נ)
police officer	ʃoter	שוֹטֵר (ז)
police station	taxanat miʃtara	תַחֲנַת מִשטָרָה (נ)
billy club	ala	אַלָה (נ)
bullhorn	megafon	מֶגָפוֹן (ז)
patrol car	na'yedet	נַייָדֶת (נ)
siren	tsofar	צוֹפָר (ז)
to turn on the siren	lehaf'il tsofar	לְהַפעִיל צוֹפָר
siren call	tsfira	צפִירָה (נ)
crime scene	zirat 'peʃa	זִירַת פֶּשַע (נ)
witness	ed	עֵד (ז)
freedom	'xofeʃ	חוֹפֶש (ז)
accomplice	ʃutaf	שוּתָף (ז)
to flee (vi)	lehixave	לְהֵיחָבֵא
trace (to leave a ~)	akev	עָקֵב (ז)

121. Police. Law. Part 2

search (investigation)	xipus	חִיפּוּש (ז)
to look for ...	lexapes	לְחַפֵּש
suspicion	xaʃad	חָשָד (ז)
suspicious (e.g., ~ vehicle)	xaʃud	חָשוּד
to stop (cause to halt)	la'atsor	לַעֲצוֹר
to detain (keep in custody)	la'atsor	לַעֲצוֹר
case (lawsuit)	tik	תִיק (ז)
investigation	xakira	חֲקִירָה (נ)

detective	balaʃ	בַּלָשׁ (ז)
investigator	xoker	חוֹקֵר (ז)
hypothesis	haʃara	הַשְׁעָרָה (נ)

motive	me'ni'a	מֵנִיעַ (ז)
interrogation	xakira	חֲקִירָה (נ)
to interrogate (vt)	laxkor	לַחְקוֹר
to question (~ neighbors, etc.)	letaʃel	לְתַשְׁאֵל
check (identity ~)	bdika	בְּדִיקָה (נ)

round-up	matsod	מָצוֹד (ז)
search (~ warrant)	xipus	חִיפּוּשׂ (ז)
chase (pursuit)	mirdaf	מִרְדָּף (ז)
to pursue, to chase	lirdof axarei	לִרְדּוֹף אַחֲרֵי
to track (a criminal)	la'akov axarei	לַעֲקוֹב אַחֲרֵי

arrest	ma'asar	מַאֲסָר (ז)
to arrest (sb)	le'esor	לֶאֱסוֹר
to catch (thief, etc.)	lilkod	לִלְכּוֹד
capture	lexida	לְכִידָה (נ)

document	mismax	מִסְמָך (ז)
proof (evidence)	hoxaxa	הוֹכָחָה (נ)
to prove (vt)	leho'xiax	לְהוֹכִיחַ
footprint	akev	עָקֵב (ז)
fingerprints	tvi'ot etsba'ot	טְבִיעוֹת אֶצְבָּעוֹת (נ"ר)
piece of evidence	re'aya	רְאָיָה (נ)

alibi	'alibi	אָלִיבִּי (ז)
innocent (not guilty)	xaf mi'peʃa	חַף מִפֶּשַׁע
injustice	i 'tsedek	אִי צֶדֶק (ז)
unjust, unfair (adj)	lo tsodek	לֹא צוֹדֵק

criminal (adj)	plili	פְּלִילִי
to confiscate (vt)	lehaxrim	לְהַחְרִים
drug (illegal substance)	sam	סַם (ז)
weapon, gun	'neʃek	נֶשֶׁק (ז)
to disarm (vt)	lifrok mi'neʃek	לִפְרוֹק מִנֶּשֶׁק
to order (command)	lifkod	לִפְקוֹד
to disappear (vi)	lehe'alem	לְהֵיעָלֵם

law	xok	חוֹק (ז)
legal, lawful (adj)	xuki	חוּקִי
illegal, illicit (adj)	'bilti xuki	בִּלְתִּי חוּקִי

| responsibility (blame) | axrayut | אַחְרָיוּת (נ) |
| responsible (adj) | axrai | אַחְרַאִי |

NATURE

The Earth. Part 1

122. Outer space

space	χalal	חָלָל (ז)
space (as adj)	ʃel χalal	שֶׁל חָלָל
outer space	χalal χitson	חָלָל חִיצוֹן (ז)
world	olam	עוֹלָם (ז)
universe	yekum	יְקוּם (ז)
galaxy	ga'laksya	גָלַקסיָה (נ)
star	koχav	כּוֹכָב (ז)
constellation	tsvir koχavim	צבִיר כּוֹכָבִים (ז)
planet	koχav 'leχet	כּוֹכָב לֶכֶת (ז)
satellite	lavyan	לוִויָן (ז)
meteorite	mete'orit	מֶטָאוֹרִיט (ז)
comet	koχav ʃavit	כּוֹכָב שָׁבִיט (ז)
asteroid	aste'ro'id	אַסטרוֹאִיד (ז)
orbit	maslul	מַסלוּל (ז)
to revolve (~ around the Earth)	lesovev	לְסוֹבֵב
atmosphere	atmos'fera	אַטמוֹספֶרָה (נ)
the Sun	'ʃemeʃ	שֶׁמֶשׁ (נ)
solar system	ma'a'reχet ha'ʃemeʃ	מַעֲרֶכֶת הַשֶׁמֶשׁ (נ)
solar eclipse	likui χama	לִיקוּי חַמָה (ז)
the Earth	kadur ha''arets	כַּדוּר הָאָרֶץ (ז)
the Moon	ya'reaχ	יָרֵחַ (ז)
Mars	ma'adim	מַאֲדִים (ז)
Venus	'noga	נוֹגַהּ (ז)
Jupiter	'tsedek	צֶדֶק (ז)
Saturn	ʃabtai	שַׁבּתַאי (ז)
Mercury	koχav χama	כּוֹכָב חַמָה (ז)
Uranus	u'ranus	אוּרָנוּס (ז)
Neptune	neptun	נֶפּטוּן (ז)
Pluto	'pluto	פּלוּטוֹ (ז)
Milky Way	ʃvil haχalav	שבִיל הָחָלָב (ז)
Great Bear (Ursa Major)	duba gdola	דוּבָּה גדוֹלָה (נ)

North Star	koxav hatsafon	כּוֹכַב הַצָּפוֹן (ז)
Martian	toʃav ma'adim	תּוֹשַׁב מָאֲדִים (ז)
extraterrestrial (n)	xutsan	חוּצָן (ז)
alien	xaizar	חַייָזָר (ז)
flying saucer	tsa'laxat me'o'fefet	צַלַחַת מְעוֹפֶפֶת (נ)

spaceship	xalalit	חֲלָלִית (נ)
space station	taxanat xalal	תַחֲנַת חָלָל (נ)
blast-off	hamra'a	הַמְרָאָה (נ)

engine	ma'no'a	מָנוֹעַ (ז)
nozzle	nexir	נְחִיר (ז)
fuel	'delek	דֶלֶק (ז)

cockpit, flight deck	'kokpit	קוֹקפִּיט (ז)
antenna	an'tena	אַנטֶנָה (נ)
porthole	eʃnav	אֶשׁנָב (ז)
solar panel	'luax so'lari	לוּחַ סוֹלָרִי (ז)
spacesuit	xalifat xalal	חֲלִיפַת חָלָל (נ)

| weightlessness | 'xoser miʃkal | חוֹסֶר מִשׁקָל (ז) |
| oxygen | xamtsan | חַמצָן (ז) |

| docking (in space) | agina | עֲגִינָה (נ) |
| to dock (vi, vt) | la'agon | לַעֲגוֹן |

observatory	mitspe koxavim	מִצפֶּה כּוֹכָבִים (ז)
telescope	teleskop	טֶלֶסקוֹפּ (ז)
to observe (vt)	litspot, lehaʃkif	לִצפּוֹת, לְהַשׁקִיף
to explore (vt)	laxkor	לַחקוֹר

123. The Earth

the Earth	kadur ha''arets	כַּדוּר הָאָרֶץ (ז)
the globe (the Earth)	kadur ha''arets	כַּדוּר הָאָרֶץ (ז)
planet	koxav 'lexet	כּוֹכַב לֶכֶת (ז)

atmosphere	atmos'fera	אַטמוֹספֶרָה (נ)
geography	ge'o'grafya	גֵיאוֹגרַפיָה (נ)
nature	'teva	טֶבַע (ז)

globe (table ~)	'globus	גלוֹבּוּס (ז)
map	mapa	מַפָּה (נ)
atlas	'atlas	אַטלָס (ז)

Europe	ei'ropa	אֵירוֹפָּה (נ)
Asia	'asya	אַסיָה (נ)
Africa	'afrika	אַפרִיקָה (נ)
Australia	ost'ralya	אוֹסטרַליָה (נ)
America	a'merika	אָמֶרִיקָה (נ)

North America	a'merika hatsfonit	אָמֶרִיקָה הַצְפוֹנִית (נ)
South America	a'merika hadromit	אָמֶרִיקָה הַדְרוֹמִית (נ)
Antarctica	ya'beʃet an'tarktika	יַבֶּשֶׁת אַנְטָארקטִיקָה (נ)
the Arctic	'arktika	אַרקטִיקָה (נ)

124. Cardinal directions

north	tsafon	צָפוֹן (ז)
to the north	tsa'fona	צָפוֹנָה
in the north	batsafon	בַּצָפוֹן
northern (adj)	tsfoni	צפוֹנִי
south	darom	דָרוֹם (ז)
to the south	da'roma	דָרוֹמָה
in the south	badarom	בַּדָרוֹם
southern (adj)	dromi	דרוֹמִי
west	ma'arav	מַעֲרָב (ז)
to the west	ma'a'rava	מַעֲרָבָה
in the west	bama'arav	בַּמַעֲרָב
western (adj)	ma'aravi	מַעֲרָבִי
east	mizraχ	מִזְרָח (ז)
to the east	miz'raχa	מִזְרָחָה
in the east	bamizraχ	בַּמִזְרָח
eastern (adj)	mizraχi	מִזְרָחִי

125. Sea. Ocean

sea	yam	יָם (ז)
ocean	ok'yanos	אוֹקיָאנוֹס (ז)
gulf (bay)	mifrats	מִפְרָץ (ז)
straits	meitsar	מֵיצָר (ז)
land (solid ground)	yabaʃa	יַבָּשָׁה (נ)
continent (mainland)	ya'beʃet	יַבֶּשֶׁת (נ)
island	i	אִי (ז)
peninsula	χatsi i	חֲצִי אִי (ז)
archipelago	arχipelag	אַרכִיפֶּלָג (ז)
bay, cove	mifrats	מִפְרָץ (ז)
harbor	namal	נָמָל (ז)
lagoon	la'guna	לָגוּנָה (נ)
cape	kef	כֵּף (ז)
atoll	atol	אָטוֹל (ז)
reef	ʃunit	שׁוּנִית (נ)

coral	almog	אַלמוֹג (ז)
coral reef	ʃunit almogim	שוֹנִית אַלמוֹגִים (נ)
deep (adj)	amok	עָמוֹק
depth (deep water)	'omek	עוֹמֶק (ז)
abyss	tehom	תְהוֹם (נ)
trench (e.g., Mariana ~)	maxteʃ	מַכתֵש (ז)
current (Ocean ~)	'zerem	זֶרֶם (ז)
to surround (bathe)	lehakif	לְהַקִיף
shore	xof	חוֹף (ז)
coast	xof yam	חוֹף יָם (ז)
flow (flood tide)	ge'ut	גֵאוּת (נ)
ebb (ebb tide)	'ʃefel	שֶפֶל (ז)
shoal	sirton	שִׂרטוֹן (ז)
bottom (~ of the sea)	karka'it	קַרקָעִית (נ)
wave	gal	גַל (ז)
crest (~ of a wave)	pisgat hagal	פִּסגַת הַגַל (נ)
spume (sea foam)	'ketsef	קֶצֶף (ז)
storm (sea storm)	sufa	סוּפָה (נ)
hurricane	hurikan	הוּרִיקָן (ז)
tsunami	tsu'nami	צוּנָאמִי (ז)
calm (dead ~)	'roga	רוֹגַע (ז)
quiet, calm (adj)	ʃalev	שָלֵו
pole	'kotev	קוֹטֶב (ז)
polar (adj)	kotbi	קוֹטבִּי
latitude	kav 'roxav	קַו רוֹחַב (ז)
longitude	kav 'orex	קַו אוֹרֶך (ז)
parallel	kav 'roxav	קַו רוֹחַב (ז)
equator	kav hamaʃve	קַו הַמַשווֶה (ז)
sky	ʃa'mayim	שָמַיִם (ז״ר)
horizon	'ofek	אוֹפֶק (ז)
air	avir	אַווִיר (ז)
lighthouse	migdalor	מִגדַלוֹר (ז)
to dive (vi)	litslol	לִצלוֹל
to sink (ab. boat)	lit'bo'a	לִטבּוֹעַ
treasures	otsarot	אוֹצָרוֹת (ז״ר)

126. Seas' and Oceans' names

Atlantic Ocean	ha'ok'yanus ha'at'lanti	הָאוֹקיָינוֹס הָאַטלַנטִי (ז)
Indian Ocean	ha'ok'yanus ha'hodi	הָאוֹקיָינוֹס הַהוֹדִי (ז)

| Pacific Ocean | ha'ok'yanus haʃaket | הָאוֹקיָינוֹס הַשָׁקֵט (ז) |
| Arctic Ocean | ok'yanos ha'keraχ hatsfoni | אוֹקיָינוֹס הַקֶּרַח הַצפוֹנִי (ז) |

Black Sea	hayam haʃaχor	הַיָם הַשָׁחוֹר (ז)
Red Sea	yam suf	יַם סוּף (ז)
Yellow Sea	hayam hatsahov	הַיָם הַצָהוֹב (ז)
White Sea	hayam halavan	הַיָם הַלָבָן (ז)

Caspian Sea	hayam ha'kaspi	הַיָם הַכַּספִּי (ז)
Dead Sea	yam ha'melaχ	יַם הַמֶלַח (ז)
Mediterranean Sea	hayam hatiχon	הַיָם הַתִיכוֹן (ז)

| Aegean Sea | hayam ha'e'ge'i | הַיָם הָאֶגָאִי (ז) |
| Adriatic Sea | hayam ha'adri'yati | הַיָם הָאַדרִיָאתִי (ז) |

Arabian Sea	hayam ha'aravi	הַיָם הָעֲרָבִי (ז)
Sea of Japan	hayam haya'pani	הַיָם הַיַפָּנִי (ז)
Bering Sea	yam 'bering	יַם בֶּרִינג (ז)
South China Sea	yam sin hadromi	יַם סִין הַדרוֹמִי (ז)

Coral Sea	yam ha'almogim	יַם הָאַלמוֹגִים (ז)
Tasman Sea	yam tasman	יַם טַסמַן (ז)
Caribbean Sea	hayam haka'ribi	הַיָם הַקָרִיבִּי (ז)

| Barents Sea | yam 'barents | ים בָּרֶנץ (ז) |
| Kara Sea | yam 'kara | יַם קָאַרָה (ז) |

North Sea	hayam hatsfoni	הַיָם הַצפוֹנִי (ז)
Baltic Sea	hayam ha'balti	הַיָם הַבָּלטִי (ז)
Norwegian Sea	hayam hanor'vegi	הַיָם הַנוֹרבֶגִי (ז)

127. Mountains

mountain	har	הַר (ז)
mountain range	'reχes harim	רֶכֶס הָרִים (ז)
mountain ridge	'reχes har	רֶכֶס הַר (ז)

summit, top	pisga	פִּסגָה (נ)
peak	pisga	פִּסגָה (נ)
foot (~ of the mountain)	margelot	מַרגְלוֹת (נ"ר)
slope (mountainside)	midron	מִדרוֹן (ז)

volcano	har 'ga'aʃ	הַר גַעַש (ז)
active volcano	har 'ga'aʃ pa'il	הַר גַעַש פָּעִיל (ז)
dormant volcano	har 'ga'aʃ radum	הַר גַעַש רָדוּם (ז)

eruption	hitpartsut	הִתפָּרצוּת (נ)
crater	lo'a	לוֹעַ (ז)
magma	megama	מָגמָה (נ)
lava	'lava	לָאבָה (נ)

molten (~ lava)	lohet	לוֹהֵט
canyon	kanyon	קַנְיוֹן (ז)
gorge	gai	גַיְא (ז)
crevice	'beka	בֶּקַע (ז)
abyss (chasm)	tehom	תְהוֹם (נ)
pass, col	ma'avar harim	מַעֲבַר הָרִים (ז)
plateau	rama	רָמָה (נ)
cliff	tsuk	צוּק (ז)
hill	giv'a	גִבְעָה (נ)
glacier	karxon	קַרְחוֹן (ז)
waterfall	mapal 'mayim	מַפַּל מַיִם (ז)
geyser	'geizer	גֵייזֶר (ז)
lake	agam	אֲגַם (ז)
plain	miʃor	מִישׁוֹר (ז)
landscape	nof	נוֹף (ז)
echo	hed	הֵד (ז)
alpinist	metapes harim	מְטַפֵּס הָרִים (ז)
rock climber	metapes sla'im	מְטַפֵּס סְלָעִים (ז)
to conquer (in climbing)	lixboʃ	לִכְבּוֹשׁ
climb (an easy ~)	tipus	טִיפּוּס (ז)

128. Mountains names

The Alps	harei ha''alpim	הָרֵי הָאַלְפִּים (ז״ר)
Mont Blanc	mon blan	מוֹן בְּלָאן (ז)
The Pyrenees	pire'ne'im	פִּירֶנֵאִים (ז״ר)
The Carpathians	kar'patim	קַרְפָּטִים (ז״ר)
The Ural Mountains	harei ural	הָרֵי אוּרָל (ז״ר)
The Caucasus Mountains	harei hakavkaz	הָרֵי הַקַוְוקָז (ז״ר)
Mount Elbrus	elbrus	אֶלְבְּרוּס (ז)
The Altai Mountains	harei altai	הָרֵי אַלְטַאי (ז״ר)
The Tian Shan	tyan ʃan	טְיָאן שָׁאן (ז)
The Pamir Mountains	harei pamir	הָרֵי פָּאמִיר (ז״ר)
The Himalayas	harei hehima'laya	הָרֵי הֶהִימָלָאיָה (ז״ר)
Mount Everest	everest	אֶוֶורֶסְט (ז)
The Andes	harei ha''andim	הָרֵי הָאַנְדִים (ז״ר)
Mount Kilimanjaro	kiliman'dʒaro	קִילִימַנְגָ'רוֹ (ז)

129. Rivers

river	nahar	נָהָר (ז)
spring (natural source)	ma'ayan	מַעְיָן (ז)

riverbed (river channel)	afik	אָפִיק (ז)
basin (river valley)	agan nahar	אַגַן נָהָר (ז)
to flow into …	lehiʃapex	לְהִישָׁפֵךְ
tributary	yuval	יוּבַל (ז)
bank (of river)	xof	חוֹף (ז)
current (stream)	'zerem	זֶרֶם (ז)
downstream (adv)	bemorad hanahar	בְּמוֹרַד הַנָהָר
upstream (adv)	bema'ale hanahar	בְּמַעֲלֵה הַזָרֶם
inundation	hatsafa	הֲצָפָה (נ)
flooding	ʃitafon	שִׁיטָפוֹן (ז)
to overflow (vi)	la'alot al gdotav	לַעֲלוֹת עַל גְדוֹתָיו
to flood (vt)	lehatsif	לְהָצִיף
shallow (shoal)	sirton	שִׂרטוֹן (ז)
rapids	'eʃed	אֶשֶׁד (ז)
dam	'sexer	סֶכֶר (ז)
canal	te'ala	תְעָלָה (נ)
reservoir (artificial lake)	ma'agar 'mayim	מַאֲגַר מַיִם (ז)
sluice, lock	ta 'ʃayit	תָא שַׁיִט (ז)
water body (pond, etc.)	ma'agar 'mayim	מַאֲגַר מַיִם (ז)
swamp (marshland)	bitsa	בִּיצָה (נ)
bog, marsh	bitsa	בִּיצָה (נ)
whirlpool	me'ar'bolet	מְעַרבּוֹלֶת (נ)
stream (brook)	'naxal	נַחַל (ז)
drinking (ab. water)	ʃel ʃtiya	שֶׁל שתִיָיה
fresh (~ water)	metukim	מְתוּקִים
ice	'kerax	קֶרַח (ז)
to freeze over (ab. river, etc.)	likpo	לִקפּוֹא

130. Rivers' names

Seine	hasen	הַסֶן (ז)
Loire	lu'ar	לוּאָר (ז)
Thames	'temza	תָמזָה (ז)
Rhine	hrain	הרַיין (ז)
Danube	da'nuba	דָנוּבָּה (ז)
Volga	'volga	וֹולגָה (ז)
Don	nahar don	נָהָר דוֹן (ז)
Lena	'lena	לֶנָה (ז)
Yellow River	hvang ho	הוֹאנג הוֹ (ז)

Yangtze	yangtse	יַאנגצָה (ז)
Mekong	mekong	מָקוֹנג (ז)
Ganges	'ganges	גַנגֶס (ז)

Nile River	'nilus	נִילוּס (ז)
Congo River	'kongo	קוֹנגוֹ (ז)
Okavango River	ok'vango	אוֹקבָנגוֹ (ז)
Zambezi River	zam'bezi	זַמבֶּזִי (ז)
Limpopo River	limpopo	לִימפּוֹפּוֹ (ז)
Mississippi River	misi'sipi	מִיסִיסִיפִּי (ז)

131. Forest

| forest, wood | 'ya'ar | יַעַר (ז) |
| forest (as adj) | ʃel 'ya'ar | שֶל יַעַר |

thick forest	avi ha'ya'ar	עָבִי הַיַעַר (ז)
grove	xurʃa	חוּרשָה (נ)
forest clearing	ka'raxat 'ya'ar	קָרַחַת יַעַר (נ)

| thicket | svax | סבָך (ז) |
| scrubland | 'siax | שִׂיחַ (ז) |

| footpath (troddenpath) | ʃvil | שבִיל (ז) |
| gully | 'emek tsar | עֵמֶק צַר (ז) |

tree	ets	עֵץ (ז)
leaf	ale	עָלֶה (ז)
leaves (foliage)	alva	עַלווָה (נ)

fall of leaves	ʃa'lexet	שַלֶכֶת (נ)
to fall (ab. leaves)	linʃor	לִנשוֹר
top (of the tree)	tsa'meret	צָמֶרֶת (נ)

branch	anaf	עָנָף (ז)
bough	anaf ave	עָנָף עָבֶה (ז)
bud (on shrub, tree)	nitsan	נִיצָן (ז)
needle (of pine tree)	'maxat	מַחַט (נ)
pine cone	itstrubal	אִצטרוּבָּל (ז)

hollow (in a tree)	xor ba'ets	חוֹר בָּעֵץ (ז)
nest	ken	קֵן (ז)
burrow (animal hole)	mexila	מְחִילָה (נ)

trunk	'geza	גֶזַע (ז)
root	'ʃoreʃ	שוֹרֶש (ז)
bark	klipa	קלִיפָּה (נ)
moss	taxav	טַחַב (ז)
to uproot (remove trees or tree stumps)	la'akor	לַעֲקוֹר

to chop down	lixrot	לִכְרוֹת
to deforest (vt)	levare	לְבָרֵא
tree stump	'gedem	גֶּדֶם (ז)

campfire	medura	מְדוּרָה (נ)
forest fire	srefa	שְׂרֵיפָה (נ)
to extinguish (vt)	lexabot	לְכַבּוֹת

forest ranger	ʃomer 'ya'ar	שׁוֹמֵר יַעַר (ז)
protection	ʃmira	שְׁמִירָה (נ)
to protect (~ nature)	liʃmor	לִשְׁמוֹר
poacher	tsayad lelo reʃut	צַיָּיד לְלֹא רְשׁוּת (ז)
steel trap	mal'kodet	מַלְכּוֹדֶת (נ)

| to gather, to pick (vt) | lelaket | לְלַקֵּט |
| to lose one's way | lit'ot | לִתְעוֹת |

132. Natural resources

natural resources	otsarot 'teva	אוֹצְרוֹת טֶבַע (ז"ר)
minerals	mine'ralim	מִינֶרָלִים (ז"ר)
deposits	mirbats	מִרְבָּץ (ז)
field (e.g., oilfield)	mirbats	מִרְבָּץ (ז)

to mine (extract)	lixrot	לִכְרוֹת
mining (extraction)	kriya	כְּרִיָּיה (נ)
ore	afra	עַפְרָה (נ)
mine (e.g., for coal)	mixre	מִכְרֶה (ז)
shaft (mine ~)	pir	פִּיר (ז)
miner	kore	כּוֹרֶה (ז)

| gas (natural ~) | gaz | גָּז (ז) |
| gas pipeline | tsinor gaz | צִינּוֹר גָּז (ז) |

oil (petroleum)	neft	נֵפְט (ז)
oil pipeline	tsinor neft	צִינּוֹר נֵפְט (ז)
oil well	be'er neft	בְּאֵר נֵפְט (נ)
derrick (tower)	migdal ki'duax	מִגְדַּל קִידּוּחַ (ז)
tanker	mexalit	מֵיכָלִית (נ)

sand	xol	חוֹל (ז)
limestone	'even gir	אֶבֶן גִּיר (נ)
gravel	xatsats	חָצָץ (ז)
peat	kavul	כָּבוּל (ז)
clay	tit	טִיט (ז)
coal	pexam	פֶּחָם (ז)

iron (ore)	barzel	בַּרְזֶל (ז)
gold	zahav	זָהָב (ז)
silver	'kesef	כֶּסֶף (ז)

nickel	'nikel	נִיקֶל (ז)
copper	ne'xoʃet	נְחוֹשֶׁת (נ)
zinc	avats	אָבָץ (ז)
manganese	mangan	מַנגָן (ז)
mercury	kaspit	כַּספִּית (נ)
lead	o'feret	עוֹפֶרֶת (נ)
mineral	mineral	מִינָרָל (ז)
crystal	gaviʃ	גָבִיש (ז)
marble	'ʃayiʃ	שַׁיִש (ז)
uranium	u'ranyum	אוּרָניוּם (ז)

The Earth. Part 2

133. Weather

weather	'mezeg avir	מֶזֶג אֲוִויר (ז)
weather forecast	taxazit 'mezeg ha'avir	תַחֲזִית מֶזֶג הָאֲוִויר (נ)
temperature	tempera'tura	טֶמפֶּרָטוּרָה (נ)
thermometer	madxom	מַדחוֹם (ז)
barometer	ba'rometer	בָּרוֹמֶטֶר (ז)
humid (adj)	lax	לַח
humidity	laxut	לַחוּת (נ)
heat (extreme ~)	xom	חוֹם (ז)
hot (torrid)	xam	חַם
it's hot	xam	חַם
it's warm	xamim	חָמִים
warm (moderately hot)	xamim	חָמִים
it's cold	kar	קַר
cold (adj)	kar	קַר
sun	'ʃemeʃ	שֶמֶש (נ)
to shine (vi)	lizhor	לִזהוֹר
sunny (day)	ʃimʃi	שִמשִי
to come up (vi)	liz'roax	לִזרוֹחַ
to set (vi)	liʃ'ko'a	לִשקוֹעַ
cloud	anan	עָנָן (ז)
cloudy (adj)	me'unan	מְעוּנָן
rain cloud	av	עָב (ז)
somber (gloomy)	sagriri	סַגרִירִי
rain	'geʃem	גֶשֶם (ז)
it's raining	yored 'geʃem	יוֹרֵד גֶשֶם
rainy (~ day, weather)	gaʃum	גָשוּם
to drizzle (vi)	letaftef	לְטַפטֵף
pouring rain	matar	מָטָר (ז)
downpour	mabul	מַבּוּל (ז)
heavy (e.g., ~ rain)	xazak	חָזָק
puddle	ʃlulit	שלוּלִית (נ)
to get wet (in rain)	lehitratev	לְהִתרַטֵב
fog (mist)	arapel	עֲרָפֶל (ז)
foggy	me'urpal	מְעוּרפָּל

snow	'ʃeleg	שֶׁלֶג (ז)
it's snowing	yored 'ʃeleg	יוֹרֵד שֶׁלֶג

134. Severe weather. Natural disasters

thunderstorm	sufat re'amim	סוּפַת רְעָמִים (נ)
lightning (~ strike)	barak	בָּרָק (ז)
to flash (vi)	livhok	לִבהוֹק
thunder	'ra'am	רַעַם (ז)
to thunder (vi)	lir'om	לִרעוֹם
it's thundering	lir'om	לִרעוֹם
hail	barad	בָּרָד (ז)
it's hailing	yored barad	יוֹרֵד בָּרָד
to flood (vt)	lehatsif	לְהָצִיף
flood, inundation	ʃitafon	שִׁיטָפוֹן (ז)
earthquake	re'idat adama	רְעִידַת אֲדָמָה (נ)
tremor, quake	re'ida	רְעִידָה (נ)
epicenter	moked	מוֹקֵד (ז)
eruption	hitpartsut	הִתפָּרצוּת (נ)
lava	'lava	לָאבָה (נ)
twister	hurikan	הוּרִיקָן (ז)
tornado	tor'nado	טוֹרנָדוֹ (ז)
typhoon	taifun	טַייפוּן (ז)
hurricane	hurikan	הוּרִיקָן (ז)
storm	sufa	סוּפָה (נ)
tsunami	tsu'nami	צוּנָאמִי (ז)
cyclone	tsiklon	צִיקלוֹן (ז)
bad weather	sagrir	סַגרִיר (ז)
fire (accident)	srefa	שְׂרֵיפָה (נ)
disaster	ason	אָסוֹן (ז)
meteorite	mete'orit	מֶטָאוֹרִיט (ז)
avalanche	ma'polet ʃlagim	מַפּוֹלֶת שלָגִים (נ)
snowslide	ma'polet ʃlagim	מַפּוֹלֶת שלָגִים (נ)
blizzard	sufat ʃlagim	סוּפַת שלָגִים (נ)
snowstorm	sufat ʃlagim	סוּפַת שלָגִים (נ)

Fauna

135. Mammals. Predators

predator	xayat 'teref	חַיַּית טֶרֶף (ז)
tiger	'tigris	טִיגְרִיס (ז)
lion	arye	אַרְיֵה (ז)
wolf	ze'ev	זְאֵב (ז)
fox	ʃu'al	שׁוּעָל (ז)
jaguar	yagu'ar	יָגוּאָר (ז)
leopard	namer	נָמֵר (ז)
cheetah	bardelas	בַּרְדְּלָס (ז)
black panther	panter	פֶּנְתֵּר (ז)
puma	'puma	פּוּמָה (נ)
snow leopard	namer 'ʃeleg	נָמֵר שֶׁלֶג (ז)
lynx	ʃunar	שׁוּנָר (ז)
coyote	ze'ev ha'aravot	זְאֵב הָעֲרָבוֹת (ז)
jackal	tan	תַּן (ז)
hyena	tsa'vo'a	צָבוֹעַ (ז)

136. Wild animals

animal	'ba'al xayim	בַּעַל חַיִּים (ז)
beast (animal)	xaya	חַיָּה (נ)
squirrel	sna'i	סְנָאִי (ז)
hedgehog	kipod	קִיפּוֹד (ז)
hare	arnav	אַרְנָב (ז)
rabbit	ʃafan	שָׁפָן (ז)
badger	girit	גִּירִית (נ)
raccoon	dvivon	דְּבִיבוֹן (ז)
hamster	oger	אוֹגֵר (ז)
marmot	mar'mita	מַרְמִיטָה (נ)
mole	xafar'peret	חֲפַרְפֶּרֶת (נ)
mouse	axbar	עַכְבָּר (ז)
rat	xulda	חוּלְדָּה (נ)
bat	atalef	עֲטַלֵּף (ז)
ermine	hermin	הֶרְמִין (ז)
sable	tsobel	צוֹבֶּל (ז)

marten	dalak	דָּלָק (ז)
weasel	xamus	חָמוּס (ז)
mink	xorfan	חוֹרְפָן (ז)

| beaver | bone | בּוֹנֶה (ז) |
| otter | lutra | לוּטְרָה (נ) |

horse	sus	סוּס (ז)
moose	ayal hakore	אַיָּל הַקּוֹרֵא (ז)
deer	ayal	אַיָּל (ז)
camel	gamal	גָּמָל (ז)

bison	bizon	בִּיזוֹן (ז)
aurochs	bizon ei'ropi	בִּיזוֹן אֵירוֹפִּי (ז)
buffalo	te'o	תְּאוֹ (ז)

zebra	'zebra	זֶבְּרָה (נ)
antelope	anti'lopa	אַנְטִילוֹפָּה (נ)
roe deer	ayal hakarmel	אַיָּל הַכַּרְמֶל (ז)
fallow deer	yaxmur	יַחְמוּר (ז)
chamois	ya'el	יָעֵל (ז)
wild boar	xazir bar	חֲזִיר בָּר (ז)

whale	livyatan	לִוְיָתָן (ז)
seal	'kelev yam	כֶּלֶב יָם (ז)
walrus	sus yam	סוּס יָם (ז)
fur seal	dov yam	דּוֹב יָם (ז)
dolphin	dolfin	דּוֹלְפִין (ז)

bear	dov	דּוֹב (ז)
polar bear	dov 'kotev	דּוֹב קוֹטֶב (ז)
panda	'panda	פַּנְדָּה (נ)

monkey	kof	קוֹף (ז)
chimpanzee	ʃimpanze	שִׁימְפַּנְזֶה (ז)
orangutan	orang utan	אוֹרַנְג־אוּטָן (ז)
gorilla	go'rila	גּוֹרִילָּה (נ)
macaque	makak	מָקָק (ז)
gibbon	gibon	גִּיבּוֹן (ז)

elephant	pil	פִּיל (ז)
rhinoceros	karnaf	קַרְנַף (ז)
giraffe	dʒi'rafa	גִּ׳ירָפָה (נ)
hippopotamus	hipopotam	הִיפּוֹפּוֹטָם (ז)

| kangaroo | 'kenguru | קֶנְגוּרוּ (ז) |
| koala (bear) | ko''ala | קוֹאֶלָה (ז) |

mongoose	nemiya	נְמִיָּה (נ)
chinchilla	tʃin'tʃila	צִ׳ינְצִ׳ילָה (נ)
skunk	bo'eʃ	בּוֹאֵשׁ (ז)
porcupine	darban	דַּרְבָּן (ז)

137. Domestic animals

cat	χatula	חָתוּלָה (נ)
tomcat	χatul	חָתוּל (ז)
dog	'kelev	כֶּלֶב (ז)
horse	sus	סוּס (ז)
stallion (male horse)	sus harba'a	סוּס הַרְבָּעָה (ז)
mare	susa	סוּסָה (נ)
cow	para	פָּרָה (נ)
bull	ʃor	שׁוֹר (ז)
ox	ʃor	שׁוֹר (ז)
sheep (ewe)	kivsa	כִּבְשָׂה (נ)
ram	'ayil	אַיִל (ז)
goat	ez	עֵז (נ)
billy goat, he-goat	'tayiʃ	תַּיִשׁ (ז)
donkey	χamor	חֲמוֹר (ז)
mule	'pered	פֶּרֶד (ז)
pig, hog	χazir	חֲזִיר (ז)
piglet	χazarzir	חֲזַרְזִיר (ז)
rabbit	arnav	אַרְנָב (ז)
hen (chicken)	tarne'golet	תַּרְנְגוֹלֶת (נ)
rooster	tarnegol	תַּרְנְגוֹל (ז)
duck	barvaz	בַּרְוָז (ז)
drake	barvaz	בַּרְוָז (ז)
goose	avaz	אֲוָז (ז)
tom turkey, gobbler	tarnegol 'hodu	תַּרְנְגוֹל הֹדוּ (ז)
turkey (hen)	tarne'golet 'hodu	תַּרְנְגוֹלֶת הֹדוּ (נ)
domestic animals	χayot 'bayit	חַיּוֹת בַּיִת (נ״ר)
tame (e.g., ~ hamster)	mevuyat	מְבוּיָת
to tame (vt)	levayet	לְבַיֵּת
to breed (vt)	lehar'bi'a	לְהַרְבִּיעַ
farm	χava	חַוָּה (נ)
poultry	ofot 'bayit	עוֹפוֹת בַּיִת (נ״ר)
cattle	bakar	בָּקָר (ז)
herd (cattle)	'eder	עֵדֶר (ז)
stable	urva	אוּרְוָה (נ)
pigpen	dir χazirim	דִּיר חֲזִירִים (ז)
cowshed	'refet	רֶפֶת (נ)
rabbit hutch	arnaviya	אַרְנָבִיָּה (נ)
hen house	lul	לוּל (ז)

138. Birds

bird	tsipor	צִיפּוֹר (נ)
pigeon	yona	יוֹנָה (נ)
sparrow	dror	דרוֹר (ז)
tit (great tit)	yargazi	יַרגָזִי (ז)
magpie	orev neχalim	עוֹרֵב נְחָלִים (ז)

raven	orev ʃaχor	עוֹרֵב שָׁחוֹר (ז)
crow	orev afor	עוֹרֵב אָפוֹר (ז)
jackdaw	ka'ak	קָאָק (ז)
rook	orev hamizra	עוֹרֵב הַמִזרָע (ז)

duck	barvaz	בַּרווָז (ז)
goose	avaz	אֲווָז (ז)
pheasant	pasyon	פַּסיוֹן (ז)

eagle	'ayit	עַיִט (ז)
hawk	nets	נֵץ (ז)
falcon	baz	בַּז (ז)
vulture	ozniya	עוֹזנִייָה (נ)
condor (Andean ~)	kondor	קוֹנדוֹר (ז)

swan	barbur	בַּרבּוּר (ז)
crane	agur	עָגוּר (ז)
stork	χasida	חֲסִידָה (נ)

parrot	'tuki	תוּכִּי (ז)
hummingbird	ko'libri	קוֹלִיבּרִי (ז)
peacock	tavas	טַווָס (ז)

ostrich	bat ya'ana	בַּת יַעֲנָה (נ)
heron	anafa	אֲנָפָה (נ)
flamingo	fla'mingo	פּלָמִינגוֹ (ז)
pelican	saknai	שַׂקנַאי (ז)

nightingale	zamir	זָמִיר (ז)
swallow	snunit	סנוּנִית (נ)

thrush	kiχli	קִיכלִי (ז)
song thrush	kiχli mezamer	קִיכלִי מְזַמֵר (ז)
blackbird	kiχli ʃaχor	קִיכלִי שָׁחוֹר (ז)

swift	sis	סִיס (ז)
lark	efroni	עֶפרוֹנִי (ז)
quail	slav	שׂלָיו (ז)

woodpecker	'neker	נֶקֶר (ז)
cuckoo	kukiya	קוּקִייָה (נ)
owl	yanʃuf	יַנשוּף (ז)
eagle owl	'oaχ	אוֹחַ (ז)

wood grouse	seχvi 'ya'ar	שְׂכווי יַעַר (ז)
black grouse	seχvi	שְׂכווי (ז)
partridge	χogla	חוֹגלָה (נ)

starling	zarzir	זַרזִיר (ז)
canary	ka'narit	קָנָרִית (נ)
hazel grouse	seχvi haya'arot	שְׂכווי הַיְעָרוֹת (ז)
chaffinch	paroʃ	פָּרוֹש (ז)
bullfinch	admonit	אַדמוֹנִית (נ)

seagull	ʃaχaf	שַחַף (ז)
albatross	albatros	אַלבַּטרוֹס (ז)
penguin	pingvin	פִּינגווִין (ז)

139. Fish. Marine animals

bream	avroma	אַברוֹמָה (נ)
carp	karpiyon	קַרפִּיוֹן (ז)
perch	'okunus	אוֹקוּנוּס (ז)
catfish	sfamnun	שׂפַמנוּן (ז)
pike	ze'ev 'mayim	זְאֵב מַיִם (ז)

| salmon | 'salmon | סַלמוֹן (ז) |
| sturgeon | χidkan | חִדקָן (ז) |

herring	ma'liaχ	מָלִיחַ (ז)
Atlantic salmon	iltit	אִילתִית (נ)
mackerel	makarel	מָקָרָל (ז)
flatfish	dag moʃe ra'benu	דַג מֹשֶה רַבֵּנוּ (ז)

zander, pike perch	amnun	אַמנוּן (ז)
cod	ʃibut	שִיבּוּט (ז)
tuna	'tuna	טוּנָה (נ)
trout	forel	פוֹרֶל (ז)

eel	tslofaχ	צלוֹפַח (ז)
electric ray	trisanit	תרִיסָנִית (נ)
moray eel	mo'rena	מוֹרֶנָה (נ)
piranha	pi'ranya	פִּירָניָה (נ)

shark	kariʃ	כָּרִיש (ז)
dolphin	dolfin	דוֹלפִין (ז)
whale	livyatan	לִווייָתָן (ז)

crab	sartan	סַרטָן (ז)
jellyfish	me'duza	מֶדוּזָה (נ)
octopus	tamnun	תַמנוּן (ז)

| starfish | koχav yam | כּוֹכַב יָם (ז) |
| sea urchin | kipod yam | קִיפוֹד יָם (ז) |

seahorse	suson yam	סוסון יָם (ז)
oyster	tsidpa	צְדָפָה (נ)
shrimp	xasilon	חָסִילון (ז)
lobster	'lobster	לוֹבּסטֶר (ז)
spiny lobster	'lobster kotsani	לוֹבּסטֶר קוֹצָנִי (ז)

140. Amphibians. Reptiles

snake	naxaʃ	נָחָש (ז)
venomous (snake)	arsi	אַרסִי
viper	'tsefa	צֶפַע (ז)
cobra	'peten	פֶּתֶן (ז)
python	piton	פִּיתוֹן (ז)
boa	xanak	חֲנָק (ז)
grass snake	naxaʃ 'mayim	נָחָש מַיִם (ז)
rattle snake	ʃfifon	שפִיפוֹן (ז)
anaconda	ana'konda	אֲנָקוֹנדָה (נ)
lizard	leta'a	לְטָאָה (נ)
iguana	igu"ana	אִיגוּאָנָה (נ)
monitor lizard	'koax	כּוֹחַ (ז)
salamander	sala'mandra	סָלָמַנדרָה (נ)
chameleon	zikit	זִיקִית (נ)
scorpion	akrav	עַקרָב (ז)
turtle	tsav	צָב (ז)
frog	tsfar'de'a	צפַרדֵעַ (נ)
toad	karpada	קַרפָּדָה (נ)
crocodile	tanin	תַנִין (ז)

141. Insects

insect, bug	xarak	חָרָק (ז)
butterfly	parpar	פַּרפַּר (ז)
ant	nemala	נְמָלָה (נ)
fly	zvuv	זבוב (ז)
mosquito	yatuʃ	יַתוּש (ז)
beetle	xipuʃit	חִיפּוּשִית (נ)
wasp	tsir'a	צִרעָה (נ)
bee	dvora	דבוֹרָה (נ)
bumblebee	dabur	דָבוּר (ז)
gadfly (botfly)	zvuv hasus	זבוב הַסוּס (ז)
spider	akaviʃ	עַכָּבִיש (ז)
spiderweb	kurei akaviʃ	קוּרֵי עַכָּבִיש (ז"ר)

dragonfly	ʃapirit	שְׁפִּירִית (נ)
grasshopper	χagav	חָגָב (ז)
moth (night butterfly)	aʃ	עָשׁ (ז)

cockroach	makak	מַקָּק (ז)
tick	kartsiya	קַרְצִיָּה (נ)
flea	par'oʃ	פַּרְעוֹשׁ (ז)
midge	yavχuʃ	יַבחוּשׁ (ז)

locust	arbe	אַרְבֶּה (ז)
snail	χilazon	חִילָזוֹן (ז)
cricket	tsartsar	צְרָצַר (ז)
lightning bug	gaχlilit	גַּחְלִילִית (נ)
ladybug	parat moʃe ra'benu	פָּרַת מֹשֶׁה רַבֵּנוּ (נ)
cockchafer	χipuʃit aviv	חִיפּוּשִׁית אָבִיב (נ)

leech	aluka	עֲלוּקָה (נ)
caterpillar	zaχal	זַחַל (ז)
earthworm	to'la'at	תּוֹלַעַת (נ)
larva	'deren	דָּרֶן (ז)

Flora

142. Trees

tree	ets	עֵץ (ז)
deciduous (adj)	naʃir	נָשִׁיר
coniferous (adj)	maxtani	מַחטָנִי
evergreen (adj)	yarok ad	יָרוֹק עַד
apple tree	ta'puax	תַפּוּחַ (ז)
pear tree	agas	אַגָס (ז)
sweet cherry tree	gudgedan	גוּדגְדָן (ז)
sour cherry tree	duvdevan	דוּבדְבָן (ז)
plum tree	ʃezif	שְׁזִיף (ז)
birch	ʃadar	שְׁדָר (ז)
oak	alon	אַלוֹן (ז)
linden tree	'tilya	טִילִיָה (נ)
aspen	aspa	אַסְפָּה (נ)
maple	'eder	אֶדֶר (ז)
spruce	a'ʃuax	אַשׁוּחַ (ז)
pine	'oren	אוֹרֶן (ז)
larch	arzit	אַרזִית (נ)
fir tree	a'ʃuax	אַשׁוּחַ (ז)
cedar	'erez	אֶרֶז (ז)
poplar	tsaftsefa	צַפצָפָה (נ)
rowan	ben xuzrar	בֶּן־חוּזרָר (ז)
willow	arava	עֲרָבָה (נ)
alder	alnus	אַלנוּס (ז)
beech	aʃur	אָשׁוּר (ז)
elm	bu'kitsa	בּוּקִיצָה (נ)
ash (tree)	mela	מֵילָה (נ)
chestnut	armon	עַרמוֹן (ז)
magnolia	mag'nolya	מַגנוֹלִיָה (נ)
palm tree	'dekel	דֶקֶל (ז)
cypress	broʃ	בְּרוֹשׁ (ז)
mangrove	mangrov	מַנגרוֹב (ז)
baobab	ba'obab	בָּאוֹבָּב (ז)
eucalyptus	eika'liptus	אֵיקָלִיפּטוּס (ז)
sequoia	sek'voya	סְקוֹוִיָה (נ)

143. Shrubs

bush	'siax	שִׂיחַ (ז)
shrub	'siax	שִׂיחַ (ז)
grapevine	'gefen	גֶּפֶן (ז)
vineyard	'kerem	כֶּרֶם (ז)
raspberry bush	'petel	פֶּטֶל (ז)
blackcurrant bush	'siax dumdemaniyot ʃxorot	שִׂיחַ דּוּמְדְּמָנִיוֹת שְׁחוֹרוֹת (ז)
redcurrant bush	'siax dumdemaniyot adumot	שִׂיחַ דּוּמְדְּמָנִיוֹת אֲדוּמּוֹת (ז)
gooseberry bush	xazarzar	חֲזַרְזָר (ז)
acacia	ʃita	שִׁיטָה (נ)
barberry	berberis	בֶּרְבֶּרִיס (ז)
jasmine	yasmin	יַסְמִין (ז)
juniper	ar'ar	עַרְעָר (ז)
rosebush	'siax vradim	שִׂיחַ וְרָדִים (ז)
dog rose	'vered bar	וֶרֶד בַּר (ז)

144. Fruits. Berries

fruit	pri	פְּרִי (ז)
fruits	perot	פֵּירוֹת (ז"ר)
apple	ta'puax	תַּפּוּחַ (ז)
pear	agas	אַגָּס (ז)
plum	ʃezif	שְׁזִיף (ז)
strawberry (garden ~)	tut sade	תּוּת שָׂדֶה (ז)
sour cherry	duvdevan	דּוּבְדְּבָן (ז)
sweet cherry	gudgedan	גּוּדְגְּדָן (ז)
grape	anavim	עֲנָבִים (ז"ר)
raspberry	'petel	פֶּטֶל (ז)
blackcurrant	dumdemanit ʃxora	דּוּמְדְּמָנִית שְׁחוֹרָה (נ)
redcurrant	dumdemanit aduma	דּוּמְדְּמָנִית אֲדוּמָּה (נ)
gooseberry	xazarzar	חֲזַרְזָר (ז)
cranberry	xamutsit	חֲמוּצִית (נ)
orange	tapuz	תַּפּוּז (ז)
mandarin	klemen'tina	קְלֶמֶנְטִינָה (נ)
pineapple	'ananas	אֲנָנָס (ז)
banana	ba'nana	בַּנָנָה (נ)
date	tamar	תָּמָר (ז)
lemon	limon	לִימוֹן (ז)
apricot	'miʃmeʃ	מִשְׁמֵשׁ (ז)

peach	afarsek	אֲפַרְסֵק (ז)
kiwi	'kivi	קִיוִוי (ז)
grapefruit	eʃkolit	אֶשְׁכּוֹלִית (נ)
berry	garger	גַּרְגֵּר (ז)
berries	gargerim	גַּרְגְּרִים (ז"ר)
cowberry	uχmanit aduma	אוּכְמָנִית אֲדוּמָה (נ)
wild strawberry	tut 'ya'ar	תּוּת יַעַר (ז)
bilberry	uχmanit	אוּכְמָנִית (נ)

145. Flowers. Plants

flower	'peraχ	פֶּרַח (ז)
bouquet (of flowers)	zer	זֵר (ז)
rose (flower)	'vered	וֶרֶד (ז)
tulip	tsiv'oni	צִבְעוֹנִי (ז)
carnation	tsi'poren	צִיפּוֹרֶן (ז)
gladiolus	glad'yola	גְלָדִיוֹלָה (נ)
cornflower	dganit	דְגָנִיָה (נ)
harebell	pa'amonit	פַּעֲמוֹנִית (נ)
dandelion	ʃinan	שִׁינָן (ז)
camomile	kamomil	קָמוֹמִיל (ז)
aloe	alvai	אֲלוַוי (ז)
cactus	'kaktus	קַקְטוּס (ז)
rubber plant, ficus	'fikus	פִּיקוּס (ז)
lily	ʃoʃana	שׁוֹשַׁנָה (נ)
geranium	ge'ranyum	גֶּרַנְיוּם (ז)
hyacinth	yakinton	יָקִינְטוֹן (ז)
mimosa	mi'moza	מִימוֹזָה (נ)
narcissus	narkis	נַרְקִיס (ז)
nasturtium	'kova hanazir	כּוֹבַע הַנָּזִיר (ז)
orchid	saχlav	סַחְלָב (ז)
peony	admonit	אַדְמוֹנִית (נ)
violet	sigalit	סִיגָּלִית (נ)
pansy	amnon vetamar	אַמְנוֹן וְתָמָר (ז)
forget-me-not	ziχ'rini	זִכְרִינִי (ז)
daisy	marganit	מַרְגָּנִית (נ)
poppy	'pereg	פֶּרֶג (ז)
hemp	ka'nabis	קָנַאבִּיס (ז)
mint	'menta	מֶנְתָה (נ)
lily of the valley	zivanit	זִיווָנִית (נ)
snowdrop	ga'lantus	גָּלַנְטוּס (ז)

nettle	sirpad	סִרְפָּד (ז)
sorrel	χum'a	חוּמְעָה (נ)
water lily	nufar	נוּפָר (ז)
fern	ʃaraχ	שָׁרָךְ (ז)
lichen	χazazit	חֲזָזִית (נ)
greenhouse (tropical ~)	χamama	חָמָמָה (נ)
lawn	midʃa'a	מִדְשָׁאָה (נ)
flowerbed	arugat praχim	עֲרוּגַת פְּרָחִים (נ)
plant	'tsemaχ	צֶמַח (ז)
grass	'deʃe	דֶּשֶׁא (ז)
blade of grass	giv'ol 'esev	גִבְעוֹל עֵשֶׂב (ז)
leaf	ale	עָלֶה (ז)
petal	ale ko'teret	עָלֶה כּוֹתֶרֶת (ז)
stem	giv'ol	גִבְעוֹל (ז)
tuber	'pka'at	פְּקַעַת (נ)
young plant (shoot)	'nevet	נֶבֶט (ז)
thorn	kots	קוֹץ (ז)
to blossom (vi)	lif'roaχ	לִפְרוֹחַ
to fade, to wither	linbol	לִנְבּוֹל
smell (odor)	'reaχ	רֵיחַ (ז)
to cut (flowers)	ligzom	לִגְזוֹם
to pick (a flower)	liktof	לִקְטוֹף

146. Cereals, grains

grain	tvu'a	תְבוּאָה (נ)
cereal crops	dganim	דְּגָנִים (ז״ר)
ear (of barley, etc.)	ʃi'bolet	שִׁיבּוֹלֶת (נ)
wheat	χita	חִיטָה (נ)
rye	ʃifon	שִׁיפוֹן (ז)
oats	ʃi'bolet ʃu'al	שִׁיבּוֹלֶת שׁוּעָל (נ)
millet	'doχan	דּוֹחַן (ז)
barley	se'ora	שְׂעוֹרָה (נ)
corn	'tiras	תִירָס (ז)
rice	'orez	אוֹרֶז (ז)
buckwheat	ku'semet	כּוּסֶמֶת (נ)
pea plant	afuna	אֲפוּנָה (נ)
kidney bean	ʃu'it	שְׁעוּעִית (נ)
soy	'soya	סוֹיָה (נ)
lentil	adaʃim	עֲדָשִׁים (נ״ר)
beans (pulse crops)	pol	פּוֹל (ז)

COUNTRIES. NATIONALITIES

147. Western Europe

Europe	ei'ropa	אֵירוֹפָּה (נ)
European Union	ha'iχud ha'eiro'pe'i	הָאִיחוּד הָאֵירוֹפִּי (ז)
Austria	'ostriya	אוֹסְטְרְיָה (נ)
Great Britain	bri'tanya hagdola	בְּרִיטַנְיָה הַגְדוֹלָה (נ)
England	'angliya	אַנְגְלִיָה (נ)
Belgium	'belgya	בֶּלְגִיָה (נ)
Germany	ger'manya	גֶרְמַנְיָה (נ)
Netherlands	'holand	הוֹלַנְד (נ)
Holland	'holand	הוֹלַנְד (נ)
Greece	yavan	יָוָן (נ)
Denmark	'denemark	דֶנֶמַרק (נ)
Ireland	'irland	אִירלַנְד (נ)
Iceland	'island	אִיסְלַנְד (נ)
Spain	sfarad	סְפָרַד (נ)
Italy	i'talya	אִיטַלְיָה (נ)
Cyprus	kafrisin	קַפְרִיסִין (נ)
Malta	'malta	מַלְטָה (נ)
Norway	nor'vegya	נוֹרבֶגיָה (נ)
Portugal	portugal	פּוֹרטוּגָל (נ)
Finland	'finland	פִינלַנד (נ)
France	tsarfat	צָרְפַת (נ)
Sweden	'ʃvedya	שבֶדיָה (נ)
Switzerland	'ʃvaits	שוַוייץ (נ)
Scotland	'skotland	סקוֹטלַנד (נ)
Vatican	vatikan	וָתִיקָן (ז)
Liechtenstein	liχtenʃtain	לִיכְטֶנשטֵיין (נ)
Luxembourg	luksemburg	לוּקסֶמבּוּרג (נ)
Monaco	mo'nako	מוֹנָקוֹ (נ)

148. Central and Eastern Europe

Albania	al'banya	אַלבַּנְיָה (נ)
Bulgaria	bul'garya	בּוּלגַרְיָה (נ)
Hungary	hun'garya	הוּנגַרְיָה (נ)

Latvia	'latviya	לַטבִיָה (נ)
Lithuania	'lita	לִיטָא (נ)
Poland	polin	פּוֹלִין (נ)
Romania	ro'manya	רוֹמַניָה (נ)
Serbia	'serbya	סֶרבִיָה (נ)
Slovakia	slo'vakya	סלוֹבָקיָה (נ)
Croatia	kro''atya	קרוֹאָטיָה (נ)
Czech Republic	'tʃexya	צ'כיָה (נ)
Estonia	es'tonya	אֶסטוֹניָה (נ)
Bosnia and Herzegovina	'bosniya	בּוֹסניָה (נ)
Macedonia (Republic of ~)	make'donya	מָקדוֹניָה (נ)
Slovenia	slo'venya	סלוֹבֶניָה (נ)
Montenegro	monte'negro	מוֹנטֶנֶגרוֹ (נ)

149. Former USSR countries

Azerbaijan	azerbaidʒan	אָזֶרבֵּייגָ'ן (נ)
Armenia	ar'menya	אַרמֶניָה (נ)
Belarus	'belarus	בֶּלָרוּס (נ)
Georgia	'gruzya	גרוּזיָה (נ)
Kazakhstan	kazaχstan	קַזַחסטַן (נ)
Kirghizia	kirgizstan	קִירגִיזסטָן (נ)
Moldova, Moldavia	mol'davya	מוֹלדָביָה (נ)
Russia	'rusya	רוּסיָה (נ)
Ukraine	uk'rayna	אוּקרָאִינָה (נ)
Tajikistan	tadʒikistan	טָגִ'יקִיסטָן (נ)
Turkmenistan	turkmenistan	טוּרקמָנִיסטָן (נ)
Uzbekistan	uzbekistan	אוּזבָּקִיסטָן (נ)

150. Asia

Asia	'asya	אָסיָה (נ)
Vietnam	vyetnam	וְיֶטנָאם (נ)
India	'hodu	הוֹדוּ (נ)
Israel	yisra'el	יִשׂרָאֵל (נ)
China	sin	סִין (נ)
Lebanon	levanon	לְבָנוֹן (נ)
Mongolia	mon'golya	מוֹנגוֹליָה (נ)
Malaysia	ma'lezya	מָלֶזיָה (נ)
Pakistan	pakistan	פָּקִיסטָן (נ)

Saudi Arabia	arav hasa'udit	עֲרָב הַסְעוּדִית (נ)
Thailand	'tailand	תָאִילֶנְד (נ)
Taiwan	taivan	טַייוָון (נ)
Turkey	'turkiya	טוּרקִיָה (נ)
Japan	yapan	יַפָן (נ)

Afghanistan	afganistan	אַפגָנִיסטָן (נ)
Bangladesh	bangladeʃ	בַּנגלָדֶש (נ)
Indonesia	indo'nezya	אִינדוֹנֶזיָה (נ)
Jordan	yarden	יַרדֵן (נ)

Iraq	irak	עִירָאק (נ)
Iran	iran	אִירָן (נ)
Cambodia	kam'bodya	קַמבּוֹדיָה (נ)
Kuwait	kuveit	כּוּוֵית (נ)

Laos	la'os	לָאוֹס (נ)
Myanmar	miyanmar	מִיאַנמָר (נ)
Nepal	nepal	נֶפָּאל (נ)
United Arab Emirates	ixud ha'emi'royot ha'araviyot	אִיחוּד הָאֱמִירוֹיוֹת הָעֲרָבִיוֹת (ז)

Syria	'surya	סוּריָה (נ)
Palestine	falastin	פָּלֶסטִין (נ)
South Korea	ko'rei'a hadromit	קוֹרֵיאָה הַדרוֹמִית (נ)
North Korea	ko'rei'a hatsfonit	קוֹרֵיאָה הַצפוֹנִית (נ)

151. North America

United States of America	artsot habrit	אַרצוֹת הַבּרִית (נ"ר)
Canada	'kanada	קָנָדָה (נ)
Mexico	'meksiko	מָקסִיקוֹ (נ)

152. Central and South America

Argentina	argen'tina	אַרגֶנטִינָה (נ)
Brazil	brazil	בּרָזִיל (נ)
Colombia	ko'lombya	קוֹלוֹמבִּיָה (נ)
Cuba	'kuba	קוּבָּה (נ)
Chile	'tʃile	צִ'ילֶה (נ)

Bolivia	bo'livya	בּוֹלִיביָה (נ)
Venezuela	venetsu''ela	וֶנֶצוּאֶלָה (נ)
Paraguay	paragvai	פָּרָגוּוַאי (נ)
Peru	peru	פֶּרוּ (נ)

| Suriname | surinam | סוּרִינָאם (נ) |
| Uruguay | urugvai | אוּרוּגוּוַאי (נ) |

Ecuador	ekvador	אֶקְוָדוֹר (נ)
The Bahamas	iyey ba'hama	אָיֵי בָּהָאמָה (ז"ר)
Haiti	ha''iti	הָאִיטִי (נ)

Dominican Republic	hare'publika hadomeni'kanit	הָרֶפּוּבְּלִיקָה הַדּוֹמִינִיקָנִית (נ)
Panama	pa'nama	פָּנָמָה (נ)
Jamaica	dʒa'maika	גִ'מַייקָה (נ)

153. Africa

Egypt	mits'rayim	מִצְרַיִם (נ)
Morocco	ma'roko	מָרוֹקוֹ (נ)
Tunisia	tu'nisya	טוּנִיסְיָה (נ)

Ghana	'gana	גָאנָה (נ)
Zanzibar	zanzibar	זַנזִיבָּר (נ)
Kenya	'kenya	קֶניָה (נ)
Libya	luv	לוּב (נ)
Madagascar	madagaskar	מָדָגַסקָר (ז)

Namibia	na'mibya	נָמִיבּיָה (נ)
Senegal	senegal	סֶנֶגָל (נ)
Tanzania	tan'zanya	טַנזַניָה (נ)
South Africa	drom 'afrika	דרוֹם אָפרִיקָה (נ)

154. Australia. Oceania

| Australia | ost'ralya | אוֹסטרַלִיָה (נ) |
| New Zealand | nyu 'ziland | ניוּ זִילָנד (נ) |

| Tasmania | tas'manya | טַסמַניָה (נ) |
| French Polynesia | poli'nezya hatsarfatit | פּוֹלִינֶזיָה הַצָרפָתִית (נ) |

155. Cities

Amsterdam	'amsterdam	אַמסטֶרדָם (נ)
Ankara	ankara	אַנקָרָה (נ)
Athens	a'tuna	אָתוּנָה (נ)
Baghdad	bagdad	בָּגדָד (נ)
Bangkok	bangkok	בַּנגקוֹק (נ)

Barcelona	bartse'lona	בַּרצֶלוֹנָה (נ)
Beijing	beidʒing	בֵּייגִ'ינג (נ)
Beirut	beirut	בֵּירוּת (נ)
Berlin	berlin	בֶּרלִין (נ)

Bonn	bon	בּוֹן (נ)
Bordeaux	bordo	בּוֹרדוֹ (נ)
Bratislava	bratis'lava	בּרָטִיסלָאבָה (נ)
Brussels	brisel	בּרִיסֶל (נ)
Bucharest	'bukareʃt	בּוּקָרֶשט (נ)
Budapest	'budapeʃt	בּוּדָפֶּשט (נ)
Cairo	kahir	קָהִיר (נ)
Chicago	ʃi'kago	שִיקָאגוֹ (נ)
Copenhagen	kopen'hagen	קוֹפֶּנהָגֶן (נ)
Dar-es-Salaam	dar e salam	דָאר אֶ־סָלָאם (נ)
Delhi	'delhi	דֶלהִי (נ)
Dubai	dubai	דוּבַּאי (נ)
Dublin	'dablin	דַבּלִין (נ)
Düsseldorf	'diseldorf	דִיסֶלדוֹרף (נ)
Florence	fi'rentse	פִירֶנצֶה (נ)
Frankfurt	'frankfurt	פרָנקפוּרט (נ)
Geneva	ʤe'neva	ג׳נֶבָה (נ)
Hamburg	'hamburg	הַמבּוּרג (נ)
Hanoi	hanoi	הָאנוֹי (נ)
Havana	ha'vana	הָוָואנָה (נ)
Helsinki	'helsinki	הֶלסִינקִי (נ)
Hiroshima	hiro'ʃima	הִירוֹשִימָה (נ)
Hong Kong	hong kong	הוֹנג קוֹנג (נ)
Istanbul	istanbul	אִיסטַנבּוּל (נ)
Jerusalem	yeruʃa'layim	יְרוּשָלַיִם (נ)
Kolkata (Calcutta)	kol'kata	קוֹלקָטָה (נ)
Kuala Lumpur	ku''ala lumpur	קוּאָלָה לוּמפּוּר (נ)
Kyiv	'kiyev	קִייֶב (נ)
Lisbon	lisbon	לִיסבּוֹן (נ)
London	'london	לוֹנדוֹן (נ)
Los Angeles	los 'anʤeles	לוֹס אַנג׳לֶס (נ)
Lyons	li'on	לִיאוֹן (נ)
Madrid	madrid	מַדרִיד (נ)
Marseille	marsei	מַרסֵי (נ)
Mexico City	'meksiko 'siti	מֶקסִיקוֹ סִיטִי (נ)
Miami	ma'yami	מָיאָמִי (נ)
Montreal	montri'ol	מוֹנטרִיאוֹל (נ)
Moscow	'moskva	מוֹסקבָה (נ)
Mumbai (Bombay)	bombei	בּוֹמבֵּיי (נ)
Munich	'minxen	מִינכֶן (נ)
Nairobi	nai'robi	נַיירוֹבִּי (נ)
Naples	'napoli	נָפּוֹלִי (נ)
New York	nyu york	ניו יוֹרק (נ)
Nice	nis	נִיס (נ)

Oslo	'oslo	אוֹסלוֹ (נ)
Ottawa	'otava	אוֹטָוָוה (נ)
Paris	pariz	פָּרִיז (נ)
Prague	prag	פּרָאג (נ)

Rio de Janeiro	'riyo de ʒa'nero	רִיוֹ דָה זָ'נֶרוֹ (נ)
Rome	'roma	רוֹמָא (נ)
Saint Petersburg	sant 'petersburg	סָנט פֶּטֶרסבּוּרג (נ)
Seoul	se'ul	סָאוּל (נ)
Shanghai	ʃanχai	שַנחַאי (נ)

Singapore	singapur	סִינגָפּוּר (נ)
Stockholm	'stokholm	סטוֹקהוֹלם (נ)
Sydney	'sidni	סִידנִי (נ)
Taipei	taipe	טַייפֶּה (נ)
The Hague	hag	הָאג (נ)
Tokyo	'tokyo	טוֹקִיוֹ (נ)

Toronto	to'ronto	טוֹרוֹנטוֹ (נ)
Venice	ve'netsya	וֶנֶצִיָה (נ)
Vienna	'vina	וִינָה (נ)
Warsaw	'varʃa	וַרשָה (נ)
Washington	'voʃington	ווֹשִינגטוֹן (נ)

www.ingramcontent.com/pod-product-compliance
Lightning Source LLC
Chambersburg PA
CBHW070551050426
42450CB00011B/2809